Teaching American History: New Directions

Matthew T. Downey, Editor

Sponsored by
The Special Interest Group for History Teachers
The National Council for the Social Studies
Bulletin No. 67

TABLE OF CONTENTS

ABOUT THE AUTHORS — v

FOREWORD — ix

INTRODUCTION
The New History and the Classroom — 1
    MATTHEW T. DOWNEY

CHAPTER 1
The "New World" of Women's History — 5
    MARY BETH NORTON
        SUGGESTIONS FOR TEACHING WOMEN'S HISTORY

    The Obituary Paper/J. Diane Cirksena — 16

    Women's History in the "Attic Trunk"/Lois J. Barnes — 18

    Working with Quantified History: Women in the Labor Force/Anne Chapman — 19

    Women's Suffrage and the Equal Rights Amendment as Topics for Student Debates/Jan Friedel — 24

CHAPTER 2
The Family in American History — 27
    ALLAN J. LICHTMAN
        SUGGESTIONS FOR TEACHING FAMILY HISTORY

    Doing Family History Projects with High School Students/G. Galin Berrier — 40

    The Family in American Literature/Catherine W. Edwards — 42

    Teaching Family History Using Museum and Community Resources/Peter S. O'Connell — 44

    The Black Family in American History: A Classroom Lesson/Thomas L. Dynneson — 47

Library of Congress Catalog Card Number 81-86080
ISBN 0-87986-043-X
Copyright © 1982 by the
NATIONAL COUNCIL FOR THE SOCIAL STUDIES
3615 Wisconsin Avenue, N.W., Washington, DC 20016

CHAPTER 3
Social History and the Teaching of History 51
PETER N. STEARNS

SUGGESTIONS FOR TEACHING SOCIAL HISTORY

Translating Social History for the Classroom/
Linda W. Rosenzweig 64

CHAPTER 4
Industrial America's Rank and File:
Recent Trends in American Labor History 73
LEON FINK

SUGGESTIONS FOR TEACHING ABOUT INDUSTRIAL AMERICA'S RANK AND FILE

The Transformation of the Working Place:
Its Impact on the Shoemakers/Fay Metcalf 83

How the Transition from Household to
Central Shop to Factory Methods of Production
Affected Workers/Clair W. Keller 85

Labor Unions/Organizations
and the Community/D.L. Schillings 88

CHAPTER 5
Native American History: New Images and Ideas 91
LAWANA TROUT

SUGGESTIONS FOR TEACHING NATIVE AMERICAN HISTORY

Teaching Native American History:
Three Approaches/Lawana Trout 103

INDEX 113

NATIONAL COUNCIL FOR THE SOCIAL STUDIES

President
James A. Banks
University of Washington
Seattle, Washington

President-Elect
Carole L. Hahn
Emory University
Atlanta, Georgia

Vice President
Jean Craven
Albuquerque Public Schools
Albuquerque, New Mexico

Executive Director
Lynne B. Iglitzin
Washington, DC

Editor
Daniel Roselle
Washington, DC

Executive Secretary Emeritus
Merrill F. Hartshorn
Washington, DC

Board of Directors
E. Gene Barr
Donald Bragaw
Todd Clark
Ann Cotton
Maryanne Danfelser
Billie A. Day
Theodore Kaltsounis
Jacquelyn L. Lendsey
Gerald Marker
Edwin Reynolds
C. Frederick Risinger
John Rossi
Donald O. Schneider
Paul R. Shires
Lois Conley Smith
Jan L. Tucker
Frances Hagemann, *ex officio*

Publications Board
Roy Erickson, Chairperson
Gloria Contreras
Sherry Moore Malone
Shirla McClain
Edwin R. Reynolds
Donald V. Salvucci
Jean Craven, *ex officio*
Daniel Roselle, *ex officio*
Allen R. Warner, *ex officio*

ABOUT THE AUTHORS

LOIS J. BARNES teaches social studies at Western Hills High School in Frankfort, Kentucky. Her publications include "Living History in the Junior High Classroom," *The History Teacher* (August 1978), and "Increasing Student Interest in U.S. History with Recipes," *Southern Social Studies Quarterly* (Winter 1978).

G. GALIN BERRIER is Division Head of Foreign Language/Social Science at Forest View High School, Arlington Heights, Illinois. He teaches Advanced Placement United States History classes, which incorporate family and community history projects that compete in the Chicago Metro History Fair.

ANNE CHAPMAN, Academic Dean at Western Reserve Academy, Hudson, Ohio, publishes regularly on women's history and on ways to integrate the new scholarship on women into the curriculum. She is the editor of *Approaches to Women's History*, published by the American Historical Association, and is contributing editor to *Women's Studies Quarterly*.

J. DIANE CIRKSENA is currently on leave from Northfield High School, Northfield, Minnesota, to serve as director of the Women in American Culture Project, a Title IV, ESEA curriculum writing project. The new curriculum will be used both in women's studies classes and in American history survey courses.

MATTHEW T. DOWNEY, editor of this Bulletin, is Professor of History at the University of Colorado in Boulder. He has published extensively on history and social studies education and is co-author, with Fay Metcalf, of *Using Local History in the Classroom* (1982), published by the American Association for State and Local History.

THOMAS L. DYNNESON, Associate Professor at the University of Texas of the Permian Basin, has recently been a Visiting Scholar at Stanford University. He is the author of *Pre-Collegiate Anthropology: Trends and Materials* and has published some twenty articles in social studies and anthropology journals.

CATHERINE W. EDWARDS is a social studies teacher at Boulder High School, Boulder, Colorado. She has developed a course in American Studies using a humanities approach and is currently working on curriculum materials on the history of American architecture.

LEON FINK is Assistant Professor in the Department of History, University of North Carolina, Chapel Hill. He has done extensive research in working-class social history and is the author of "Politics as Social History: A Case Study of Class Conflict and Political Development in Nineteenth Century New England," *Social History* (January 1982).

JAN FRIEDEL is District Support Services Coordinator, Loess Hills Area Education Agency 13, in Council Bluffs, Iowa. She is the coordinator of teacher inservice and staff development activities for teachers in thirty-five school districts. Much of her effort is devoted to training teachers in multicultural and nonsexist education.

CLAIR W. KELLER is Professor of History and Secondary Education at Iowa State University in Ames, Iowa. He is the author of *Involving Students in the New Social Studies* (1972) and co-author of *Freedom's Trail* (1979), a junior-high American history textbook. His articles have appeared in *Social Education*, *The History Teacher*, *Social Science History*, and *Pennsylvania Magazine of History and Biography*.

ALLAN J. LICHTMAN is Professor of History at the American University in Washington, D.C. He is the author of *Your Family History* (1978), *Historians and the Living Past* (1978), and *Prejudice and the Old Politics: The Presidential Election of 1928* (1979).

FAY METCALF is a social studies teacher at Boulder High School, Boulder, Colorado, and director of the school's English as a Second Language Center. She is the author of several books and articles on local history and curriculum development and is co-author of *Using Local History in the Classroom* (1982). She has served as chairperson of the Publications Board of the National Council for the Social Studies and as a guest editor of *Social Education*.

MARY BETH NORTON is Professor of History at Cornell University, and a specialist on the American Revolution and the history of women. Her articles have appeared in the *William and Mary Quarterly*, *Signs*, and in several anthologies. She is the author of *Liberty's Daughters: The Revolutionary Experience of American Women, 1750–1800* (1980).

ABOUT THE AUTHORS

PETER S. O'CONNELL is Assistant Director of the Museum Education Department at Old Sturbridge Village, Sturbridge, Massachusetts. He coordinates the museum's teacher-training programs and has published extensively on the use of museums and historic sites in social studies education.

LINDA W. ROSENZWEIG, Assistant Professor of Education at Chatham College in Pittsburgh, is currently involved in research on the teaching of history in Britain. She is co-director of the Carnegie-Mellon Project on Social History and editor of an NCSS Bulletin entitled *Developmental Perspectives on the Social Studies* (1982).

D.L. SCHILLINGS is an instructor at Homewood-Flossmoor High School, Flossmoor, Illinois, where he has taught history for the past eleven years. He is President-Elect of the Illinois Council for the Social Studies and editor of its newsletter.

PETER N. STEARNS is Heinz Professor of History at Carnegie-Mellon University in Pittsburgh. He has published extensively in the area of social history, is editor of the *Journal of Social History*, and is co-director of the NEH-funded Project on Social History, which has created social history materials for use in the secondary schools.

LAWANA TROUT directs the Institute for American Indian History at the Newberry Library in Chicago. As Curriculum Specialist for the Newberry's Center for the History of the American Indian and as a consultant for American Indian literature and history, she has worked with secondary teachers and students in the United States Canada, Mexico, and Europe.

FOREWORD

Major public policies in our society are frequently made with little regard for history and often reflect a preoccupation with the present. When a nation pays little attention to its history, it loses much of its capacity to understand its present and to shape its future. Because of the persistent and perplexing problems that our nation and world face, we urgently need historical insights that can help us to understand our complex world and to shape alternative futures that are rooted in historical realities rather than in myths, illusions, and national fantasies.

The ahistorical character of many of our national policies and the American preoccupation with the present do not result from Americans studying very little history in the schools. American students are given larger and larger doses of history in the elementary, junior high, and high school grades. Despite the challenges that history instruction encountered during the social studies reform movements of the 1960s, history remains an important and required subject in the nation's schools. The rise of the neo-conservative and back-to-basics movements has caused history to experience a resurgence in popularity, primarily because of widely held beliefs about history's contributions to loyalty and patriotism and its factual propensity. Many newly published history textbooks are bulkier than ever, studded with American flags, and replete with patriotic biographies and facts for students to memorize.

American students spend a great deal of time studying history and memorizing historical facts and biographical trivia. Consequently, the infinitesimal impact of historical thinking on much of American public policy is related more to the nature of American society and to history instruction than to the amount of time students spend studying history. Most Americans are more present-oriented than past-oriented, in large part because of their unique historical experience. However, substantial reforms in the teaching of history are essential if our citizens are to develop more sophisticated understandings of the links between the past, present, and future; a keen sensitivity to history; and the ability to formulate complex public policies that are undergirded by sharp historical insights. To help future adult citizens to attain these attitudes, understandings, and skills, history teaching must enlighten students and help them to gain critical insights into the past and present. History teaching must help students to become reflective social critics, rather than making them unthinking consumers of a largely mythical past.

Because of the misguided back-to-basics movement now in vogue, there is a serious risk that much history teaching, rather than helping students to develop keen historical insights and understandings, will again emphasize blind patriotism, myths, and the mastery of facts. Every nation has its myths, national symbols, and heroic stories that are used to help students develop loyalty to the nation-state. This is to be expected and, presumably, these motivate developing citizens to commit themselves to the overarching idealized national values. However, socializing students into the national culture to promote cultural continuity and national solidarity should be balanced with instructional components that demystify our nation and help students to gain realistic perspectives on our nation and world. Educators should strive to attain a delicate balance between educating students to be bearers of a continuous cultural tradition and educating them to be social critics interested in social change. Both goals are important in a healthy and vigorous democracy. Cultural continuity maintains important links with a nation's past. Citizens who promote social change stir a nation's conscience and force it to work harder to actualize its idealized values.

Moreover, history instruction should not only help students to maintain links with the past and to become reflective change agents, but should also help them to view society from the perspectives of diverse groups that are important participants in the human saga. Too often, historians have spoken for the victors and the powerful, and too rarely for the vanquished, the victimized, and the powerless. Consequently, students usually studied only a fraction of the human past. Those who conquer a people cannot completely know their own history until they view it from the perspectives of those conquered. Robert K. Merton describes "insider" and "outsider" perspectives on social reality. Both insiders and outsiders claim that they alone are capable of describing reality accurately and validly. However, as Merton argues, both insider and outsider perspectives are valid and legitimate and both are needed to give us a total view of social reality. It is only when we view the Westward Movement from the perspectives of both those who "won" and "lost" the West that we can fully understand this complex series of events.

Thus, this NCSS Bulletin is both timely and important. It focuses on teaching about the histories of groups that have too often been ignored by historians and whose histories, when they were recounted at all, have been told largely from outside perspectives. Because this Bulletin focuses on women, the family, workers, Native Americans, and other people frequently neglected in American history, it will enable teachers to present their students with diverse insider and outsider perspectives on our nation's past.

FOREWORD　　　　　　　　　　　　　　　　　　　　　　　　　　　　xi

Students will find these new perspectives enlightening and engaging; and they will help young people to demystify history, gain insights into the past, develop sound public policies, and, perhaps, develop a renewed commitment to act to improve the human condition.

I wish to thank Matthew T. Downey and the other contributors for preparing this Bulletin. The Special Interest Group for History Teachers of NCSS actively participated in its development. The NCSS Publications Board and Dan Roselle and his staff have again produced another important publication. We continue to be grateful for their fine work.

James A. Banks, *President*
National Council for the Social Studies

INTRODUCTION

The New History and the Classroom

MATTHEW T. DOWNEY

THE PAST DECADE and a half has been an especially eventful period for the writing of American history. It is not simply that new books have appeared which shed new light on historical events, or that new interpretations have gained ground. Such historiographical developments are commonplace. Far more significant, new fields of historical research have emerged, and established fields are undergoing radical redefinition. American historians have also begun to exploit new research methods and nontraditional source materials. Any of these developments would be important by itself; but collectively, they have even more far-reaching implications.

The most obvious evidence of the collective impact of the new historical research is the rapid development and redefinition of the field of social history. Although never a very well-defined area of research, social history was once mainly concerned with the history of education and religion, with social reform movements, and with the social changes brought about by immigration and urbanization. As long as the field lacked any central focus or preoccupation, it remained relatively incoherent. Although these traditional topics continued to receive some attention, historians during the 1960s began to pay far more attention to the history of various groups in American society — Blacks, Hispanics, Native Americans, white ethnics, blue-collar workers, and, finally, women. Although much of this activity was a response to the civil rights movement and the accompanying rediscovery of American social and cultural diversity, it brought about a reorientation of the field of social history that lasted at least through the 1970s. By the middle of that decade, a newer and still more inclusive kind of social history was emerging, one that incorporated the private as well as the public lives of those groups of Americans. Family history, the history of childrearing and of sexual behavior, the history of leisure, and the history of health care had also become major concerns of social historians. Much of the new research fits into this ever-expanding definition of social history.

While research in social history became more inclusive than ever before, it was also undergoing some radical changes in perspective. Once mainly concerned with the careers and accomplishments of reform leaders, notable educators and churchmen, and immigrants who made good, social history began to be rewritten "from the bottom up." The emphasis shifted to the everyday lives of the "anonymous Americans." This shift has had far-reaching implications. In the neighboring field of labor history, for example, a traditional preoccupation with labor unions and union leaders has largely been replaced by a new concern for the work experience of the rank-and-file laborer.

There have also been significant departures from the white- and male-centered perspective from which American history has traditionally been written. A truly Native American history is beginning to emerge in which the white settler is no longer the central character and white-Indian relations no longer are the historians' major concern. The history of slavery is being rewritten from the perspective of the slave, revealing slavery to be a far more complex institution than historians had ever imagined. Evolving beyond its early concern with "great women," women's history has also begun to develop its own unique perspective on the past. As a result, American history, in general, is becoming more complex and far richer than before.

This Bulletin is an attempt to bring several of these new directions of American historical research to the attention of secondary school teachers. The five chapters present summaries of recent research and thoughts about such research's significance in five selected areas: women's history, family history, social history, labor history, and Native American history. These are not the only examples of new approaches to American history that might have been used. Afro-American history would have served as well as Native American history to illustrate the new perspectives that have emerged in writing the history of racial minorities. Ethnic history could have been substituted for the new labor history as an example of the growing interest in working-class social history. Unfortunately, space limitations forced us to be selective.

Each chapter is also accompanied by a bibliographical essay and a section of teaching suggestions. Both are central to the purpose of this Bulletin. The bibliographies will help guide those teachers who wish to read more extensively. The teaching suggestions will assist teachers to bridge the gap that exists between recent scholarship and classroom assignments, and between what scholars are discovering and what students are learning. The form of the teaching-suggestion section varies. In three of the chapters, classroom teachers and teacher educators have contributed brief suggestions that utilize various teaching strategies and materials. In the chapter on Native American history, Lawana Trout has described several curriculum units that she and her colleagues at the Newberry Library Center for the American Indian have developed and have used successfully in the classroom. For the chapter on social history, Linda W. Rosenzweig has described the materials and teaching strategies developed by the Project on Social History at Carnegie-Mellon University. These diverse approaches yield a potpourri of activities and suggestions for materials that teachers will find useful in translating recent historical research into classroom lessons.

What are the implications of the new research in American history for teachers and students? Potentially, it has the capacity to revitalize the teaching of history, just as it has opened new possibilities for historical scholarship. As Peter N. Stearns has written, "Social history research has long had a missionary quality, a sense of opening vast new windows onto the past. It is time to impart this same quality to history teaching." Not only has the recent research produced fascinating insights into American society, but it has illuminated areas of American life that are not usually included in history courses in the schools. The new research offers teachers the possibility of helping students construct a new definition of history, as well as new perspectives on the past.

As editor of this Bulletin, I wish to thank all those who contributed to it. The hard work and cooperation of those whose names appear as authors of chapters and teaching suggestions are very much appreciated. I would also like to thank my colleagues in the Special Interest Group for History Teachers (SIGHT) for the advice, suggestions, and support that they have given along the way. The sponsorship of this Bulletin was one of the first major undertakings of SIGHT, which was organized within the National Council for the Social Studies in 1977 to promote the interests of history teachers.

CHAPTER 1

The "New World" of Women's History

MARY BETH NORTON

AMERICAN HISTORIANS today resemble many European explorers of the late fifteenth and early sixteenth centuries: they have recently discovered that they knew little about half the world. The explorers, led by Christopher Columbus and others, rediscovered the Western hemisphere; the historians, led by Barbara Welter, Carroll Smith-Rosenberg, Ann Douglas, and others, have discovered women. Prior to the 1970s, women were generally absent from the pages of American history textbooks. The only females mentioned consistently were such individuals as Anne Hutchinson, whose religious movement nearly split the fledgling Massachusetts Bay Colony; Pocahontas, whose rescue of Captain John Smith provided a colorful romantic tale already familiar to many schoolchildren; Peggy Eaton, whose scandalous conduct helped to cause a breach between Andrew Jackson and his Vice President, John C. Calhoun; and Eleanor Roosevelt, the most active of all American First Ladies. The history presented in texts has been that of men and their worlds—politics, business, diplomacy. The history of women has been nowhere to be seen.

That has now begun to change. Thanks to the scholarly efforts of many women and men, most of them younger members of the history profession, we now know that American women have had a history that is peculiarly their own. Women, to be sure, were affected by many of the same events that had an impact on men—for example, wars and depressions—but they were affected in different ways. The wars that put men into the armies put women into the factories, and the depression that deprived many men of high-status, policy-making positions left many women still employed in their low-status, low-paying service jobs. Moreover, it has now become apparent that women's history has its own chronology, separate from that of men. The important occurrences in the feminine past have related to advances in women's education, the increasing knowledge of effective birth-control methods, improvements in household technology, opportunities for work outside the home, and others. It is, accordingly, impossible to study women within the usual political-economic-diplomatic framework of American history.

That point must be emphasized. The study of women's history involves much more than simply adding discussions of the careers of a few "great women"—such as Elizabeth Cady Stanton, Harriet Beecher Stowe, or Jane Addams—to the standard narrative of American history. It involves recasting and reconceiving the entire course of events. It involves always asking parallel, sex-differentiated questions. For example, in what ways did the experience of women on the frontier differ from that of men? Did Puritanism carry the same message for both women and men? How did the lives of nineteenth-century working-class men and women resemble or differ from each other? Did technological advances affect men and women differently? (Among the interesting instances here are the inventions of the sewing machine and the typewriter.) In short, the study of women's history involves fully integrating the new knowledge about the previously unknown half of the world (females) with that of the known, the male realm.

The task is complex. Teachers and scholars accustomed to constructing a narrative based solely on events in the lives of men must reorient their thinking to encompass women. In the process, they have to avoid three traps that await the unwary. The first is the "women as victim" trap. It is all too easy to see women chiefly as men's helpless victims, as people unable to control their own fates, and as a group always dominated by the oppressive male sex. Such a view stresses men's attitudes toward women and men's control of women's lives inside and outside of the household; and, in effect, it argues that whatever happened to women happened because of men's decisions.

The second trap is the "women as class" fallacy. This view is also easy to adopt, because in differentiating women from men, one often overlooks the need to differentiate women from each other. That is, the experiences of American women from different ethnic groups, races, and economic backgrounds may differ in ways just as marked as those in which they differ as a group from men. It is important to keep constantly in mind that any given event or trend may affect black and white women, or rich and poor women, in very different ways.

The third trap, "anachronistic analysis," is just as dangerous, and perhaps even harder to avoid than the first two. American women of the past must always be taken on their own terms, and to the greatest extent possible. Perhaps, feminists today would interpret certain circumstances as oppressive; that does not necessarily mean that historically women saw their condition in the same light. It is tempting to make categorical pronouncements on such matters.

A prime example of this problem is interpreting the effect of the removal of cloth production from the home. The introduction of steam-powered spinning and weaving machinery in the early nineteenth century freed rural women from the laborious tasks of spinning and weaving by hand. Some historians have regarded that change not as an advance for women, but, rather, as a symbol of their declining status; they argue that it turned women into consumers rather than producers and meant that women no longer made a major economic contribution to the household. At the time, however, women regarded the change as immensely liberating. Teen-aged girls (for they were the chief spinners and weavers in American households) welcomed the factories that freed them from nearly six months of full-time drudgery each year. To say that the change must be seen within the context of the times does not mean that the historian must fully and unquestioningly accept contemporary women's assessment of its impact on them. But it also means that their attitudes cannot be ignored, and that before we can reach an adequate understanding of the meaning of the shift, we must look at more than just the simple question of women's household productivity. (It is entirely possible, for example, that the women who did a smaller amount of productive work within the home were thereby freed to seek employment outside it, and that their wage contributions to the household economy more than compensated for the value of their previous work. Certainly, that is precisely what seems to have happened with the daughters of Northeastern farm families who went to work in the Lowell mills.)

With that brief introduction to some of the interpretive complexities of women's history, we can proceed to summarize the findings of recent scholarship in three broad chronological divisions: colonial and revolutionary period, nineteenth century, and twentieth century.

COLONIAL AND REVOLUTIONARY PERIOD

Traditionally, life in the English colonies in America has been viewed as something of a "golden age" for white women. The "golden age" characterization has rested on four grounds: first, a belief that the relative scarcity of women in the colonies gave them a higher status than they had had in England; second, an assertion that the most oppressive aspects of the common law were not transferred to the colonies, with the result that women's legal status improved; third, an assumption that women's vital economic contributions to the maintenance of the household gave them a status relatively equal to that of their husbands; and fourth, a belief that colonial sex-role definitions were fairly fluid, so that women, if they wished, could readily find employment outside the home.

New studies have raised serious doubts about the validity of all of these contentions, which, until recently, were accepted without question. (It is important to note here, however, that some historians still regard them as at least partially accurate. I tend to disagree with that view and believe that all four of the above commonplaces should be discarded.)

Certainly, it is beyond question that colonial women were active contributors to the survival of their households. Indeed, it was recognized by all concerned that to function properly a colonial household had to contain both a master and a mistress. The man oversaw the planting, harvesting, and possible sale of the crops; the woman handled cloth production, food preservation and preparation (including smoking meats, making butter and cheese, and regular cooking and baking), cleaning and washing, and childrearing. However, even if women's labor was crucial to the success of colonial households, that did not automatically raise their status relative to that of their husbands. After all, the labor of children, slaves, or servants was also required to maintain a colonial household (the work demands were so great that married couples could rarely subsist without some sort of help), and no one would claim that the economic significance of the labor of such persons necessarily raised their status. There is no reason to believe that male migrants to the colonies questioned the then-standard belief in women's inferiority. Indeed, there is much evidence to the contrary: like their counterparts in Europe, Anglo-American men often asserted that wives should be submissive to their husbands.

The misconception seems to have arisen from an overemphasis on the importance of women's productive capacity, a flaw that has already been noted with respect to the interpretation of the impact of the introduction of textile factories. In societies in which women have a relatively high status within the household, that status appears to depend not on their contributions of labor, but rather on their control over the distribution of the community's resources. Thus, among the Iroquois, where the tribal matriarchs nominally owned the villages' fields and women controlled the distribution of food, women had a standing higher than that in almost any other known society. In colonial America, though, men controlled the distribution of resources through their ownership of real estate and their control of any wages earned by their wives.

That brings us to the issue of women's legal status in the colonies. In English law, unmarried women had the same legal rights as men (but not the right to vote). However, the near universality of marriage in the colonies meant that few women were able to exercise those rights, except late in life after they had been widowed. Under the common law, married women were their husbands' legal dependents. They could not own property, sue or be sued, or make wills. Any property they owned prior to marriage and any children of the marriage immediately fell under their husbands' control. In most colonies, divorce was impossible to obtain.

The theory that women's legal status improved in the colonies is based on two contentions: first, that since the colonies contained few well-trained lawyers, the oppressive nature of common-law provisions was somewhat eased, chiefly through ignorance of proper procedures, rather than by design; and second, that colonial women frequently used remedies available in equity courts (for example, prenuptial agreements) to soften the worst strictures of the common law. However, recent scholarship has shown that most colonial women failed to take advantage of equity's protections and has further suggested that in some colonies ignorance of common-law provisions worked against women, rather than for them. Pennsylvania law, for instance, deprived married women of certain protections they were accorded in England.

The ability of women to work outside the home was obviously affected by their legal status. Widows composed the largest share of employed women, both because they usually had to support themselves and because a woman's earnings during marriage would have been entirely at her husband's disposal. Such working women were paid for performing essentially "female" tasks like sewing, cooking, or housekeeping. The skills necessary to run a tavern or inn (one of the most common ways in which women earned money) were similar to those of managing a household. Historians have been prone to exaggerate both the numbers and the importance of working women in the colonies, but it seems likely that no more than ten percent of the female colonial population was employed at any given time. Contrast that to more than fifty percent today. The range of jobs open to women was small, with the exception that widows occasionally continued businesses started by their husbands. Recall, in addition, that ninety percent of colonial people lived in rural areas, where the opportunities for wage-earning were scarce or nonexistent, and the probable extent of the exaggeration becomes clear.

One contention remains to be discussed: the assertion that the small proportion of women to men in the colonies benefitted the women. Throughout much of the seventeenth century, there was a surplus of men in the colonial population—men tend to outnumber women in all migrant groups—especially in the South. Thus, it is argued, men competed with each other for wives, and women were able to choose men who offered the best "deals." However, in all regions of the colonies where marriage patterns have been studied, it has been discovered that in the absence of legal restraints, such as those that forbade servants to marry, women's marriage-age was lowered dramatically when the sex ratio was highly imbalanced. An *average* marriage-age for girls of sixteen-and-a-half in one Maryland county in the late seventeenth century certainly does not imply that women were being "choosy" as they selected spouses. Indeed, it might suggest the exact opposite: that marriageable girls were being exploited by their parents and their prospective husbands.

Much research needs to be done on the subject of colonial women. Historians have barely scratched the surface of the available topics. They have done somewhat better on the revolutionary period, which for years was largely ignored, but now is beginning to be recognized as an important time of transition for women. The era from 1760 to 1820 marked the beginning of the change from preindustrial to industrial society in the United States, from English possession to American republic. Recent scholarship has shown that as they were defining the nation, American men and women also were developing new notions of womanhood. Whereas a colonial woman was defined primarily as a mistress of a household, a republican woman was defined primarily as a mother. This change occurred because Americans believed that the future of the republic—and thus, ultimately, the success of the Revolution—depended on America's "rising generation," and especially its sons. Therefore, new attention was accorded to women's role in the republic and to their relationship to the polity. Women themselves, recognizing their new standing, took an interest in politics—a topic once regarded as "beyond their sphere."

The irony was that the emphasis on the importance of motherhood (something that surely gratified women whose maternal role had previously been slighted) was eventually to become confining. The nineteenth-century ideology of woman's place argued that mothers were so crucial to a child's development, and women so essential to the running of the home, that they could not legitimately leave home except under extraordinary circumstances (such as a call from God to become a missionary to the heathen in some far-off country). Thus, a development that might originally have been interpreted as an improvement in women's status—in that it accorded to them a crucial role in childrearing—ultimately turned out to lay heavy burdens on them.

NINETEENTH CENTURY

The beginnings of the industrial age had an enormous impact on American women. Some of them became factory workers, others purchased the products of factories. Some migrated to the growing cities, along with thousands of men; by 1920, a majority of the United States' population lived in urban areas. Women, as well as men, crossed the oceans from Europe and Asia to seek new homes in the New World, increasing the nation's ethnic diversity. Girls were admitted to academies and then to colleges; and slavery, that remnant of the preindustrial age, was abolished in 1865, freeing black women and men to control their own destinies at last.

It is thus far more difficult to summarize nineteenth-century trends than to discuss those of the colonial period. Perhaps the most effective approach is to examine new scholarship in two categories: domesticity and work.

In the past, historians tended to regard "Victorian" concepts of women's role—which emphasized females' piety, purity, passionlessness, and self-sacrificing nature—with disdain. It was once simply assumed that such an ideology was imposed on women by men, without their consent; and that the "cult of true womanhood," or the "cult of domesticity," as it is generally known, was unmitigatedly "bad" for women. But in recent years, historians have begun to recognize that the cult of domesticity offered women certain benefits. For one, as already noted, it elevated the functions of motherhood. For another, it placed women on a moral plane superior to that occuped by men and gave them a special social role to fulfill as keepers of the nation's morality. By relying on that image of themselves, women were able to break the bonds of their usual domestic roles and to become active in charitable and reform societies of all sorts, from temperance to abolition to anti-prostitution campaigns.

The cult of domesticity also paradoxically helped women eventually to win the vote. At first, the women's rights movement, founded by Elizabeth Cady Stanton and others at Seneca Falls in 1848, stressed the common characteristics shared by women and men. They insisted that women should be regarded as men's equals before the law, and they split with their former allies in the antislavery movement when Republican party leaders refused to include women in the wording of the Fourteenth and Fifteenth Amendments, which gave voting rights and equal legal status to Blacks. But the suffrage movement made little headway, at least on the national level, until its female leaders started to turn domestic arguments to their advantage instead of denying their validity. Women ultimately won the vote because they convincingly contended that females would bring their "innate" domestic sensibilities to politics and that they would serve as a moral, reformist force that would improve the operations of American government.

Nineteenth-century beliefs concerning woman's nature also may have assisted women in achieving the goal of lowering their fertility. Census statistics show that whereas the average woman in 1800 bore seven children in her lifetime, the average woman in 1900 bore only three. The reduction in fertility was achieved without the aid of the pill and largely without the aid of the diaphragm and the condom, which were not used at all until near the end of the century, and which were not widely available in any event. How then was it accomplished? Historians wish they knew with certainty; but it seems likely that abstinence—the most reliable method of birth control then as now—played a major role. (Withdrawal and acidic vaginal douches were also probably quite common methods of contraception.) The notion that women felt no sexual passion undoubtedly helped to persuade couples to avoid frequent intercourse. If a man accepted the common ideal of womanhood, he would respect his wife's supposed lack of desire for sex, although he might also visit one of the city brothels that housed increasing numbers of prostitutes. (The two developments, rising rates of prostitution and the notion that "good" women failed to feel passion, went hand in hand.)

Just as the traditional view of nineteenth-century women stressed the negative effects of the cult of domesticity, so too it focused only on the lives of white middle-class housewives. Newer scholarship devotes considerable attention to the lives of working-class, immigrant, and black women—those females to whom the ideology of womanhood was never formally applied. Those were the women who worked for wages in an era when women were not expected to do so.

A number of studies show that a woman's ethnic background or race had a significant effect on the kind of employment she sought and obtained. Free black women were heavily concentrated in domestic labor, not necessarily because they preferred that work, but because employers would not hire them for other jobs. During slavery, of course, black women also had little choice of work. Most were field hands, but a considerable minority (ten to twenty percent) held skilled domestic jobs on plantations. Interestingly, after slavery was abolished, black men and women tried to organize the family's finances in such a way that the wife would not have to work in the fields. They saw her status as a common laborer as a continuing badge of slavery and attempted to avoid it at all costs. Often, they were not successful because the wages paid to black men were usually too low to support a family.

Ethnicity, too, played a role. In some ethnic groups—Mexican-Americans, for example—few women worked for wages. In others, such as Italians, women tended to take temporary, seasonal jobs or to do work that they could perform in their own homes. Irish women more often worked outside the home—in domestic service or the needle trades—than did other female immigrants, and married Polish women frequently established boarding houses that served the many unmarried male Polish immigrants who had come to America. Yet, in spite of the clichés about immigrant working-class women, the recent studies also show that a greater proportion of native-born American women, white and black, labored at paid employment than did the females of any one ethnic group.

Among the native-born women who earned wages were the daughters of some middle-class families who, offered a choice between a career and marriage, chose the former. Such women, who were educated at the first women's colleges (Mount Holyoke, Smith, and Vassar, among others) or coeducational universities (such as Cornell and the University of Michigan), became settlement-house leaders, teachers, librarians, government clerks, nurses, and the like. Since it was believed that no woman could successfully combine holding a job with raising a family, these women either worked only before marriage or deliberately chose not to marry at all. Indeed, the last decades of the nineteenth century and the first years of the twentieth saw higher percentages of never-marrying women appearing on census records than at any time before or since.

TWENTIETH CENTURY

Unfortunately, the history of twentieth-century women has been relatively neglected by scholars to date. One topic that has attracted some interest is the rise of "social feminism"; that is, a female activism based not on the characteristics women share with men, but, rather, on their sex-specific qualities. Social feminists engineered the passage of protective labor legislation for women workers (for example, restricting the amount of weight they could be required to lift, limiting their overtime, and providing for lounges and rest periods) and directed the activities of the Women's Bureau of the Department of Labor. It was once thought that feminism disappeared after the passage of the Nineteenth Amendment (women's suffrage) to the Constitution; instead, it simply took this new form in the 1920s and 1930s. For the first time, some women began to try to combine career and marriage, while others founded such volunteer societies as the Association of Southern Women for the Prevention of Lynching and the Women's Organization for National Prohibition Reform. Simultaneously, the National Women's Party, the remnant of the more militant wing of the suffrage movement, kept alive the hope of a national Equal Rights Amendment. That amendment was first introduced into Congress in 1922, but it did not win a congressional majority until fifty years later and, as this is being written, it still has not been ratified by a sufficient number of states.

A major emphasis of scholarship in modern history has been change in the private, familial realm. The electrification of the country made possible the introduction of many labor-saving devices into the home; washing machines, vacuum cleaners, irons, refrigerators, and sewing machines all made their appearance. Ironically, though, studies show that the average middle-class woman's housework burden was not significantly reduced. Her work became less physically demanding, but she now had to meet higher standards of cleanliness and order. In some ways, her work burden even increased. Instead of using laundresses, for example, a middle-class housewife was now expected to do the laundry herself. In addition, changing attitudes toward childrearing (with a greater stress on the individuality of each child and on the need for parental flexibility) required her to devote more of her time to her offspring. Thus, the time she spent in household tasks was reduced only slightly, if at all.

Finally, perhaps the most important economic trend in the twentieth-century experience of women has been the increasing numbers of wives working outside the home. In 1940, when women made up 25 percent of the labor force, only 15 percent of married women were working. The proportion of married women who sought employment leaped to 24 percent during the war, and it never returned to prewar levels, even though returning veterans took many jobs away from women. Statistically, it has now become the norm, rather than the exception, for American households to include a working mother, even when at least one child is under the age of six. The full impact of that revolution has yet to be felt, although one of the effects in some homes has been to readjust the burdens of housework by dividing it more equitably among husband, wife, and children. Still, though, traditions die hard. Most working women in the United States continue to shoulder the major responsibility for cooking and cleaning.

The history of American women thus combines dramatic change — in such areas as fertility and employment outside the home — with equally dramatic continuity. Now, just as in the seventeenth century, American women are expected to do the housework and raise the children. The study of women's experiences must accordingly include attention to both innovation and tradition. Neither factor alone is sufficient to explain how American women arrived at the position in which they find themselves in 1982.

BIBLIOGRAPHY

A good starting point for anyone interested in the theoretical issues involved in women's history is Carroll, Berenice, ed., *Liberating Women's History* (Urbana: University of Illinois Press, 1976). The two most comprehensive surveys of American women's history are Ryan, Mary P., *Womanhood in America*, 2nd ed. (New York: New Viewpoints, 1979), and Degler, Carl, *At Odds: Women and the Family in America from 1790 to the Present* (New York: Oxford University Press, 1980). Lerner, Gerda, ed., *The Female Experience in America* (Indianapolis: Bobbs-Merrill, 1976) is a superb collection of documents, usefully organized around a woman's life cycle. Books composed of important articles (which will not be cited individually because of lack of space) are Berkin, Carol, and Mary Beth Norton, eds., *Women of America: A History* (Boston: Houghton Mifflin, 1979); Cott, Nancy, and Elizabeth Pleck, eds., *A Heritage of Her Own* (New York: Simon and Schuster, 1979); Cantor, Milton, and Bruce Laurie, eds., *Class, Sex and the Woman Worker* (Westport, CT: Greenwood Press, 1977); and Harley, Sharon, and Rosalyn Terborg-Penn, eds., *The Afro-American Woman: Struggles and Images* (Port Washington, N.Y.: Kennikat Press, 1978). For further bibliographic references, mostly to articles, see the review essays on American women's history by Barbara Sicherman and Mary Beth Norton, respectively, in *Signs*, 1, no. 2 (1975), 461–85 and 5, no. 2 (1979), 324–37.

Most of the studies of women in the colonial and revolutionary eras are still found in article form (see the above works for examples and citations). However, three very recent books deal with this important subject: Koehler, Lyle, *A Search for Power: The "Weaker Sex" in Seventeenth-Century New England* (Urbana: University of Illinois Press, 1980); Norton, Mary Beth, *Liberty's Daughters: The Revolutionary Experience of American Women, 1750–1800* (Boston: Little, Brown, 1980); and Kerber, Linda, K. *Women of the Republic: Intellect and Ideology in Revolutionary America* (Chapel Hill: University of North Carolina Press, 1980).

The material on nineteenth-century women is considerably richer. The major recent books are Cott, Nancy F., *The Bonds of Womanhood: Woman's Sphere in New England, 1780–1835* (New Haven: Yale University Press, 1977); Douglas, Ann, *The Feminization of American Culture* (New York: Alfred Knopf, 1977); Dublin, Thomas, *Women at Work: The Transformation of Work and Community in Lowell, Massachusetts, 1820–1860* (New York: Columbia University Press, 1979); DuBois, Ellen, *Feminism and Suffrage: The Emergence of an Independent Women's Movement in America, 1848–1869* (Ithaca: Cornell University Press, 1978); Jeffrey, Julie Roy, *Frontier Women: The Trans-Mississippi West, 1840–1880* (New York: Hill and Wang, 1979); and Sklar, Kathryn Kish, *Catharine Beecher: A Study in American Domesticity* (New Haven: Yale University Press, 1973).

Work on the twentieth century, like that on the colonial and revolutionary periods, is often found in articles, so the works listed in the first paragraph should be consulted with care. Among the useful available books are Banner, Lois, *Women in Modern America: A History* (New York: Harcourt Brace Jovanovich, 1974); Chafe, William, *The American Woman: Her Changing Social, Economic, and Political Roles, 1920–1970* (New York: Oxford University Press, 1970); Chafe, William, *Women and Equality: Changing Patterns in American Culture* (New York: Oxford University Press, 1977); Gordon, Linda, *Woman's Body, Woman's Right: A Social History of Birth Control in America* (New York: Grossman, 1976); Lemons, J. Stanley, *The Woman Citizen: Social Feminism in the 1920s* (Urbana: University of Illinois Press, 1973); and Rothman, Sheila, *Woman's Proper Place: A History of Changing Ideals and Practices, 1870 to the Present* (New York: Basic Books, 1978).

SUGGESTIONS FOR TEACHING WOMEN'S HISTORY

The Obituary Paper

J. DIANE CIRKSENA

There are presently real difficulties in trying to introduce women's studies into the curriculum at the high school level. Most students are convinced by the time they get to high school that real history is just backward extension of the political and military conflict they hear as "news" on TV. To persuade them that social history, dominated by women and based on little internal conflict, is of primary historical value is the difficult task facing teachers. Once teachers have decided to do so, there are other problems related to materials. Most of the existing materials tend to concentrate attention on those "women worthies" who qualify for examination because they made it in a "man's" world, or they zero in primarily on the suffrage movement, as if women's only interest outside the home was related to the right to vote. Concerned secondary teachers need to avoid both of these approaches. The first alternative only adds to the conviction that there were few exceptional women, and the second negates the wide variety of the female historical experience.

The obituary paper activity described below provides secondary school teachers with a way to avoid existing inadequate materials. It can be used to trace change *and* continuity, to contrast the roles of women in two centuries, and to help students to redefine history. I have made use of an obituary paper for a number of semesters with good success, and I find that students accept the assignment with a good deal of enthusiasm. They actually write two obituaries, one for a woman in 1885 (a year selected because in Northfield that particular state census is most easily accessible) and one for themselves.

First, I have the students write their own obituaries without telling them any of the objectives for the asignment. I simply point out that the objectives will be clear at a later date, give them samples of obituaries from recent editions of the Northfield *News*, ask them to observe what an obituary usually contains, and then provide time in class for them to do a rough copy. Final manuscript copies are collected the next day, evaluated for English construction and completeness of content, and filed for further reference. The teacher can tap these particular papers for a variety of other objectives.

THE "NEW WORLD" OF WOMEN'S HISTORY

For example, I compile statistics from these papers and use them for a discussion of "life expectations," as women write them quite differently from men.

Secondly, I assign the writing of an obituary for any woman they choose from the 1885 state census, and I explain how to go about finding the necessary materials. Our public library has microfilm copies of the 1885 state census, from which students can choose a real-life person of a hundred years ago. I have them select a young woman in her twenties, and preferably someone about whom they can find other later information. Tracing later additions to this woman's family and finally her date of death may be a bit tricky, but usually students can manage to find the information from later census materials, from old issues of the Northfield *News*, or by contacting the family itself. They then construct an obituary for the woman with as much accuracy as possible. If they were unsuccessful in finding the necessary factual information, I ask them to work from statistical averages related to household size, numbers of children, and normal life expectancy. (For example, a woman who was roughly age twenty in 1885 lived in a household of five or more people, could expect to give birth to six live children, and could expect to live to the age of sixty-three.)

I do insist that male students also take a woman as a subject. For the purposes of discussion and the understanding of the learning objectives, women subjects need to be used.

Finally, with both obituaries in hand, I ask students to participate in a discussion related to contrasts between generations, including factors influencing family size, roles, and "life expectations."

Here is a list of questions which will help students compare and contrast:

1. Compared to yourself, do you think your subject lived with more or less (a) stress, (b) family pressure, (c) career choice, (d) happiness, (e) peer pressure, (f) security?

2. Has the past one hundred years tended to increase or decrease distance between the sexes? How do you know?

3. By contrasting the two obituaries, how do you think the role of women has changed in the last one hundred years?

4. If your obituary had been written about a woman who had lived in a large urban setting, how would it have been different?

Such questions are but a few of those which may evolve from the writing of the obituaries. Although the years studied may differ from community to community, this process immerses students in social history.

Women's History in the "Attic Trunk"

LOIS J. BARNES

The old attic trunk has always been a source of fascination to those who discover it and the treasures it holds. The attic trunk can be explored in the classroom, too. It is a particularly useful method to introduce students to women's history of a particular era. An attic truck from the decade of the twenties, for example, can be easily assembled to form hypotheses about the changing status of women in that decade.

The "attic trunk" for the twenties that I have constructed is a sturdy cardboard box with a hinged top covered with woodgrain-design contact paper. Although some items that I included are of general interest about the era, others relate specifically to women. The trunk is recognizable as a woman's possession. It contains original artifacts, women's accessories, and photocopies of other items, including historical documents that pertain to issues directly affecting women of the decade. Among the items and documents that I have been able to find or borrow are the following:

- High school and college yearbooks, 1923–1929
- Photocopies of John Held "flapper" drawings
- A fringed, satin flapper dress (a costume that I had made)
- Actual photographs from the era (my family's, which included family scenes, such as my grandparents and their three small children posed by the family car)
- Photocopies of magazine advertising, with emphasis on those ads directed toward women, from Blue Moon silk stockings to electrical appliances to automobiles to cigarettes and cosmetics
- An actual dress, purse, and other accessories from the period, borrowed from another teacher
- *Good Housekeeping*, April, 1920, article supporting the Sheppard-Towner Maternity Bill
- Principles of the National Birth Control League
- Editorial cartoons protesting restrictions on birth control
- Declaration of Principles of the National Women's Party, 1922
- Copy of the 1922 proposed ERA
- *Good Housekeeping*, September, 1925, containing articles debating labor laws for women
- Any popular magazine article debating ERA in the twenties

Other teachers need not limit themselves to these examples.

Once the items have been taken out of the trunk and identified, the class can be divided into groups for more thorough analysis and discussion of the significance of the items. When in groups, the students should direct their attention to answering the following kinds of questions based on the evidence from the trunk:

1. Can you detect any changes in attitudes or values during this decade?
2. What factors seem to have influenced changes in values as they occurred in the twenties?
3. In particular, how did the changes in entertainment, literature, and morality affect the development of social values? Does there appear to have been a double standard with these changes?
4. Examine the popular motion pictures of the twenties. How did they depict women?
5. Refer to the yearbooks and the movies. Do there appear to have been sexual stereotypes in the twenties?
6. What comparisons or contrasts can you make between fashion styles of students of 1923 and of students of 1929? Give examples.
7. Could changes in fashion reflect changes in attitudes by and toward women in the twenties? How?
8. Did women learn to play their roles from models provided by fashion and the media?
9. What political issues involved or interested women in the early twenties? What seem to be the reasons for these interests?
10. How valid is the concept of the "emancipation of women" when applied to the twenties? Explain.
11. What information that is not included in the trunk would you need to form a more complete profile of women in the twenties?

A great deal of preparation is involved in gathering the items needed for an attic trunk. However, once the materials are collected, they are available for future use. The interest of the students generated by this approach makes the hours of planning time well spent. Use of an attic trunk is one way to include women's history in the American history course.

Working With Quantified History: Women in the Labor Force

ANNE CHAPMAN

As a supplement to conventional texts, the eleven tables below can be used to teach skills and methods, as well as content. They are also useful for encouraging personal involvement and for stimulating questions. They can easily lead to out-of-class and interdisciplinary activities. The following suggestions are only some of the possible approaches.

To help students focus on the issues associated with women's increasing participation in the paid labor force, ask them to identify changes, continui-

Table 1: Life Expectancy and Work-Life Expectancy in Years, by Sex

	Life		Work-Life	
	F	M	F	M
1900	50.7	48.2	6.3	32.1
1940	65.9	61.2	12.1	38.2
1950	71.0	65.5	15.2	41.9
1960	73.1	66.6	20.1	41.4
1970	74.6	67.1	22.9	41.4

Source: (5) p. 106

Table 2: Composition of Households

% of all households that consist of:

	persons living alone	married couple with children	one parent with children
1960	13.1	44.1	4.4
1965	15.0	42.4	4.8
1970	17.1	40.3	5.0
1975	19.6	35.4	6.7
1979	22.2	31.7	7.3

Source: (2) p. 1

Table 3: Birth, Marriage, and Divorce Rates per 1,000 Population

	Births	Marriages	Divorces
1910	30.1	10.3	0.9
1920	27.7	12.0	1.6
1930	21.3	9.2	1.6
1940	19.4	12.1	2.0
1950	24.1	11.1	2.6
1960	23.7	8.5	2.2
1970	18.4	10.6	3.5
1978	15.3	10.3	5.1

Source: (4) p. 60

Table 4: Population per Household

1900	4.76
1910	4.54
1920	4.34
1930	4.11
1940	3.67
1950	3.37
1960	3.33
1970	3.14
1978	2.81

Sources: (2) p. 2
(3) Part I, p. 41

ties, and relationships in the statistics. The hypotheses they form, and the questions they raise, can be followed-up in discussion or through additional research. The students might consider what influenced women's decisions to take jobs and their opportunities to do so. Some variables to be examined include the labor supply (immigration) and the demand for labor (expanding economy, wars), ideology (the notion of women's proper "sphere," feminism, the child-centered family), legislation (protective legislation, equal opportunity legislation), demography (life expectancy, marriage rates, birth rates, divorce rates), technology (mechanization of work in and outside the home, contraception), financial conditions (inflation, high interest rates, credit buying), and education (legal, economic, social, psychological, availability of job-related training, sex-role stereotyping). They might also examine the effect of the increase in female employment on the economy itself (employment, retirement, wages, consumption patterns, growth of the service sector) and on the family (security, division of labor, changes in the nuturing role). For additional data and still other teaching suggestions, see A. Chapman, ed., *Approaches to Women's History* (Washington, D.C.: American Historical Association, 1979).

The advantages and disadvantages of various methods of presenting statistical data can also be explored with these tables. (For some of the pitfalls

Table 5: Occupation of the Experienced Civilian Labor Force

Type of Workers (in 1,000's)	1900	1910	1920	1930	1940	1950	1960	1970
Professional & Technical								
Total (Both sexes)	1234	1758	2283	3311	3879	5081	7335	11018
Women	434	726	1008	1482	1608	2007	2793	4398
Managers								
Total (Both sexes)	1697	2462	2803	3614	3770	5155	5489	6224
Women	74	150	191	292	414	700	794	1034
Clerical								
Total (Both sexes)	877	1987	3385	4336	4982	7232	9617	13457
Women	212	688	1614	2246	2700	4502	6497	9910
Sales								
Total (Both sexes)	1307	1755	2058	3059	3450	4133	4801	5433
Women	228	379	541	736	925	1418	1746	2097
Manual								
Total (Both sexes)	10401	14234	16974	19272	20597	24266	25617	27358
Women	1477	1914	2052	2134	2720	3685	4006	5041
Service								
Total (Both sexes)	2626	3562	3313	4772	6069	6180	7590	9591
Women	1886	2413	2063	2954	3699	3532	4780	5752
Farm								
Total (Both sexes)	10888	11533	11390	10321	8995	6953	4085	2345
Women	1008	1175	1169	908	508	601	390	222

Source: (3) Part I, pp. 139–140

---

involved in the use of statistics, see D. Huff, *How to Lie with Statistics* [New York: W.W. Norton, 1954].) Students should be encouraged to present their findings in different forms, including statistical charts and graphs. They may then be asked what is gained and what is lost in each presentation and how different presentations may influence interpretation of data. For other suggestions for using quantitative history, see S. Botein, et al., eds., *Experiments in History Teaching* (Cambridge, Mass.: Harvard-Danforth Center, 1977).

The students should also be asked to identify the kinds of questions that cannot be answered by statistics. Such source collections as R. Baxandall, et al., eds., *America's Working Women: A Documentary History, 1600 to the Present* (New York: Randon House, 1976) and N. Hoffman and F. Howe, eds., *Women Working: Stories and Poems* (Old Westbury, N.Y.: The Feminist Press, 1977) will help the students generate — and answer — questions about attitudes, feelings, and individual experiences.

Finally, raise questions with the students about the accuracy, representativeness, bias, and potential for historical significance, validity, and understanding of different kinds of historical evidence. These might include textbooks, statistics, documents, interviews, and literature. In a small way, students can learn history by doing it with the aid of statistical tables such as these.

Table 6: Changes in Women's Participation in the Labor Force

	% of women in labor force	% of wives in labor force
1800	5	N/A
1900	18	6
1910	20	11
1920	20	9
1930	22	12
1940	25	15
1950	29	24
1960	33	31
1970	38	41
1979	42	49

Note: Differences in census estimating procedures make figures above not absolutely comparable. The effect, however, is very slight.
Sources: (1) pp. 3, 23; (5) p. 99

Table 7: % of Wives with Children Under 18 in the Labor Force

1950	18.4
1955	24.0
1960	27.6
1965	32.2
1970	39.7
1975	44.9
1979	51.9

Source: (1) p. 27

Table 8: Women's Earnings as a % of Men's Earnings

1955	64
1960	61
1965	60
1970	59
1975	59
1977	59
1978	59

Source: (1) p. 52

Table 9: Women as Percentage of All Employed Persons in Each Job Category

	1976	1979
Clerical workers	79	80
Service (except private household)	58	59
Operatives	31	32
Professional & technical	42	43
Private household	97	98
Sales	43	45
Managers & administrators (non-farm)	21	25
Craft	5	6

Note: (1) For comparable 1900–1970 figures, see Table 5.
(2) In 1979, 51% of all women in the "professional occupations" category were non-college teachers or registered nurses.
Sources: (1) pp. 9–10; (5) p. 101

Table 10: Percentage of All Employed Women Doing Each Kind of Job

	1940	1950	1960	1975	1978
Total number employed women (in millions)	11.9	17.5	21.9	37.0	42.1
Clerical workers	21	26	30	35	35
Service (except private household)	11	22	15	18	21*
Operatives	18	21	15	12	11
Professional & technical	13	10	12	16	16
Private household	18	10	9	3	—
Sales	7	8	8	7	7
Managers & administrators (non-farm)	4	6	5	5	6
Craft	2	1	1	N/A	2

*includes private household

Source: (5) p. 101 (Ed. note: Figures in this table are rounded off and may not total 100% exactly.)

Table 11: Percentage Distribution of Persons by Sex and Money Income

	Income under $5,000		Income over $10,000	
	Male	Female	Male	Female
1944	94.5	99.1	1.2	0.3
1950	89.2	99.2	2.0	0.2
1960	60.9	94.6	6.1	0.2
1965	49.9	88.9	11.8	0.8
1970	38.6	77.7	26.7	3.0

Source: (3) Part I, p. 298

Sources of Tables 1-11: U.S. Department of Labor, Bureau of Labor Statistics: (1) *Perspectives on Working Women* (1980), U.S. Department of Commerce, Bureau of the Census; (2) *Household and Family Characteristics* ('79); (3) *Historical Statistics of the United States, Colonial Times to 1970* (1976); (4) *Statistical Abstracts of the United States* (1979); (5) Anne Chapman, ed., *Approaches to Women's History* (Washington, D.C.: American Historical Association, 1979).

Women's Suffrage and the Equal Rights Amendment as Topics for Student Debates

JAN FRIEDEL

The struggle for women's political rights has had two main thrusts: women's suffrage and the Equal Rights Amendment. Many people opposed passage of the Nineteenth Amendment. Other individuals and groups still oppose ratification of the Equal Rights Amendment.

A teaching strategy that I have found successful to examine and analyze the issues concerning women's political rights is a student debate. This strategy can easily be modified to accommodate different class sizes, and it is flexible in the amount of class time needed to complete the project. This activity also fosters the development of research skills and encourages active student participation, sharing, and cooperation.

In the debate, the students assume roles representative of individuals from various segments of society for the historical period concerned. For example, when studying women's suffrage, the students' roles may include a black female domestic worker, an urban social reformer, a housewife, a college-educated female, a Baptist minister, a southern Congressman, the daughter of a southern plantation owner, an abolitionist, an Italian immigrant, and a midwest farmer. The students may be given the option to represent specific individuals. When debating the Equal Rights Amendment, for example, their roles may include those of Shirley Chisholm, Phyllis Schlafly, Gloria Steinem, a Born-Again Christian, and Ronald Reagan.

The students must first investigate the intent of either women's suffrage or the Equal Rights Amendment. What legislation already exists concerning the rights specified in each? What would be the probable effects of each on American society? As a result of ratification, what changes would take place in the areas of marriage and family, employment, education, military service, and criminal justice? Biographical data on specific individuals must also be thoroughly studied to determine the effects of personal backgrounds on their positions.

Use of primary sources will be of utmost importance to the student. By using appropriate primary sources, the students will gain an understanding of the attitudes, beliefs, and values of the individuals and of the segments of society that they represent. They should also be able to present those beliefs convincingly. Such anti-suffrage arguments as "the home will go to destruction," "women will become office seekers, and there are not offices enough to go around," and "two-thirds of the church consists of women and it might unite church and state"—which at first glance may seem silly and incomprehensible — will be put into proper historical perspective. (See *Why Women Do Not Want the Ballot*.) The students will be able to accept the men and women of the past on their own terms, avoiding the trap that Mary Beth Norton calls "anachronistic analysis."

The students will quickly become aware from primary sources that not all women were in support of the Nineteenth Amendment and that not all men were opposed to it. They will also see that the same events may have affected various groups, but not in the same ways. Such documents will also help them to understand that factors such as sex, religion, race, nationality, social status, economic class, geographical region, and educational background influence one's understanding and interpretation of facts and issues. Thus, the students will avoid the "women as class" fallacy cited by Mary Beth Norton.

Based on the biographical sketches that the students write for their hypothetical characters, or the background data that they obtain on specific individuals, the students determine their characters' positions on the issue. Students are paired "pro" versus "con" for the debate, which is presented to the entire class. The audience must judge if the student espoused beliefs, values, and arguments which are consistent with the biographical data, and did so convincingly enough to persuade them to agree with his or her side of the issue. A time limit should be set for the presentation of arguments, rebuttal, and concluding remarks by each side. The teacher may devise a score sheet for each observer to record his or her reactions. The results are to be shared in an open class discussion.

As a teacher I have found these debates to be lively, informative, and sometimes emotional, and that high school students find them not only educational, but exciting as well.

BIBLIOGRAPHY

Equal Rights Amendment — A Bibliographic Study, compiled by the Equal Rights Amendment Project, Anita Miller, Project Director. Westport, Conn.: Greenwood Press, 1976.

Flexner, Eleanor, *Century of Struggle: The Women's Rights Movement in the United States*. Cambridge, Mass.: Belknap Press, 1959.

Hecker, Eugene, *A Short History of Women's Rights*. New York, N.Y.: Knickerbocker Press, 1910.

Schlafly, Phyllis, *The Power of the Positive Woman*. New Rochelle, N.Y.: Arlington House Publications, 1977.

Schellhardt, Timothy, "Interpreting ERA: Legal Experts Say Plan to Outlaw Sex Bias Is Widely Misunderstood," *Wall Street Journal*, May 16, 1979, pp. 1, 19.

Why Women Do Not Want the Ballot. North American Review Publishing Co., 1903.

CHAPTER 2

The Family in American History

ALLAN J. LICHTMAN

IN VIRTUALLY EVERY human society, past and present, the family has been the most fundamental and durable of institutions. Yet, until recently, it was ignored by historians. Only in the late 1960s did scholars begin to realize that studies of the American family could reveal much about how people lived in past times, as well as illuminate the process of historical change.

The awakening of interest in family history is part of a broader trend toward a "new social history" that seeks to reconstruct the everyday experiences of ordinary people. Rather than just the "biography of great men," or the narrative of epic events, history becomes the story of how most people lived and worked and of the values and expectations that they shared. Family history is distinguished from other work in the new social history by a focus on the family itself as a distinct institution with a major influence on the shaping of human relationships. This chapter will first describe the traditional model of American family history and then indicate how it has been refined, revised, and extended by recent research.

THE TRADITIONAL MODEL

Prior to the late 1960s, sociologists, relying upon backward projections from theory, surveys of Third World societies, and gleanings from surviving letters and diaries, had articulated the prevailing interpretation of American family history. According to this conventional wisdom, families in early America not only contained large numbers of children, but were typically extended in form, including under the same roof grandparents, parents, and children, and often collateral kin, servants, and apprentices. Scholars viewed these extended families as stable, tightly organized, dominated by patriarchal male authority, and sustained by traditionally defined roles that stifled personal initiative. Work was seen as integrated into family life, and families were viewed as self-sufficient in most of the products and services we now obtain from outside sources.

This classic family, the story goes, began to disintegrate in the nineteenth century under the pressures of industrialization and urbanization. The development of an industrial economy separated work from the home, reduced the economic importance of children, and placed a premium on individual initiative and the mobility to seek employment opportunity. Thus, couples chose to have fewer children and to form nuclear families consisting only of children and parents. Parental authority declined, traditional roles lost their meaning, and the newly powerful state stripped the family of its educational and welfare functions. Family members became increasingly absorbed in self-advancement, and bonds of romantic love came to be the main force holding families together. The dénouement of these changes, according to some authorities, is today's disintegrating family, unprotected from the ordeals of modern life and unable to satisfy the increasingly narcissistic demands of its members.[1]

Until recently, the only major exception to this account of the transformed American family was the standard interpretation of Black family life. The Black family, in this view, was doomed from the start by a system of slavery that destroyed both people's commitment to family life and their ability to maintain stable family arrangements. This version of the Black experience gained national attention in the "Moynihan Report" on the Black family submitted to President Johnson in 1965 by Harvard sociologist Daniel Patrick Moynihan, now the senior Senator from New York State. The devastations of slavery, Moynihan argued, had created a lasting "tangle of pathology" for Black families that subverted well-intentioned governmental efforts to improve their well-being in contemporary society.

The more astute sociologists recognized that their generalizations about American family history rested on the flimsiest of evidence. As William J. Goode observed in 1964, with the exception of Edmund Morgan's *The Puritan Family*, "Not a single history of the United States family would meet modern standards of historical research."[2] Since that time, however, much of the pioneering work accomplished by historians has systematically tested the traditional model of American family history.

FAMILY STRUCTURE

A major emphasis of recent scholarship has been to determine the actual structure of the family during different periods of American history. Historians have fashioned collective profiles of the families residing in particular localities by using birth, death, and marriage records to reconstruct the composition of individual families; and they have tabulated the characteristics of families listed in census returns. A major casualty of both lines of inquiry is the thesis of the historical shift from extended to nuclear families.

---

[1] For a more extended discussion of the traditional model along with appropriate references, see Rudy Ray Seward, *The American Family: A Demographic History* (Beverly Hills: Sage Publications, 1978), pp. 21–27.
[2] William J. Goode, *The Family* (Englewood Cliffs, New Jersey: Prentice-Hall, 1964), p. 105.

The nuclear family, research now shows, was the overwhelmingly prevalent family structure throughout American history, including the period prior to the burgeoning of industry. People seem to have established separate homes for themselves and their children as a matter of choice and to have expanded the family largely in response to economic necessity.[3] One recent analysis of census reports discloses that during the period of rapid industrialization, from 1850 to 1880, the proportion of three generation families actually increased from 2.4 percent to 7.3 percent.[4] In 1970, 7.2 percent of all families included three generations within the same household.

Blacks no less than whites seem to have been committed to the nuclear family form. Contrary to the traditional view, in the immediate aftermath of slavery, most Black Americans were able to establish stable, two-parent families. In the words of Herbert G. Gutman, "Enslavement was harsh and constricted the enslaved. But it did not destroy their capacity to adapt and sustain the vital familial kin associations and beliefs that served as the underpinning of a developing Afro-American culture."[5] The greatest changes in Black family life have occurred during the twentieth century, probably in reaction to the pressures of discrimination in education, housing, and employment. Between 1965 and 1977, for example, Census Bureau statistics show an increase in Black households headed by women from 24 percent to 36 percent and an increase in Black children on welfare from 14 percent to 38 percent.

These findings about the historical duration of nuclear families indicate that the individualistic values allegedly unique to modern culture may have predominated in Western society prior to the advent of an industrial economy. Other studies provide corroborating evidence. A content analysis of colonial periodicals by Herman R. Lantz and his colleagues revealed a surprising emphasis on "romantic love" and the achievement of "personal happiness" in marriage.[6] Daniel Scott Smith discovered a power struggle in Hingham, Massachusetts, between parents and children in the still-pastoral era of the eighteenth century. By the late 1700s, he found, children had succeeded in reducing parental control over their marital decisions.[7]

Francis L.K. Hsu has been especially ambitious in his efforts to trace the deep roots of American family culture. In a provocative, if speculative, essay, Hsu contends that American family life reflects an individualism that has been part of the Western heritage for thousands of years. In contrast to Asian society, Hsu maintains, Western society has always been "centrifugal

---

[3]This result is consistent with findings for pre-industrial Europe. Peter Laslett and R. Wall, eds., *Household and Family in Past Time* (New York: Cambridge University Press, 1972).

[4]Seward, *The American Family*, p. 86.

[5]Herbert G. Gutman, *The Black Family in Slavery and Freedom, 1750–1925* (New York: Pantheon Books, 1976), p. 465.

[6]Herman R. Lantz, et al., "Pre-industrial Patterns in the Colonial Families in America," *American Sociological Review* 33 (June 1968), pp. 413–26; Herman R. Lantz, R. Schmitt, and R. Herman, "The Pre-industrial Family in America: A Further Examination of Early Magazines," *American Journal of Sociology* 79 (November 1973), pp. 566–88.

[7]Daniel Scott Smith, "Parental Power and Marriage Patterns: An Analysis of Historical Trends in Hingham, Massachusetts," *Journal of Marriage and the Family* 35 (August 1973), pp. 419–28.

or outward looking" and thus characterized by "an atomistic situation in which humans become emotional islands." He notes that all the ingredients of modern American family life, including mobility, lack of reverence for parents, struggles for authority, and fragmentation of the kin group, which "social scientists claim to be the results of industrialization," can be identified in the Biblical myth of Noah and the great flood. None of these elements, however, are to be found in the Chinese counterpart of the flood myth.[8]

Just as scholars seem to have disposed of the extended family, critics began pointing to the limited relevance of pigeonholing families as either extended or nuclear. In this instant revision of the revisionists themselves, historians rightly noted that families are not static entities, but flexible living arrangements that have a life cycle of their own. Although studies may show a preponderance of nuclear families at any point in time, many of these families, at some phase of the life cycle, may have included more than just parents and children. In a study of Providence, Rhode Island, during the 1860s, Howard Chudacoff discovered that, after one year of marriage, a majority of couples who remained in the city lived either in someone else's household or in a household of their own that included boarders or relatives other than children.[9] In their study of "Urbanization and the Malleable Household," John Modell and Tamara K. Hareven noted the prevalence of boarders and lodgers in urban households of the late nineteenth and early twentieth centuries. "From a wide variety of sources," they wrote, "one gets the impression that for half a century and probably more the proportion of urban households which *at any particular time* had boarders or lodgers was between 15 and 20 percent."[10] Several studies have shown that during the nineteenth century, unlike today, the typical pattern was for elderly, widowed parents to move in with married children, rather than maintain an independent residence. The proportion of elderly widows and widowers relative to the number of households, however, was not sufficiently large to create more than a small minority of three generational families.[11]

Historians have also noted that the classification of families according to household composition slights the importance of nonresident kin who may play vital roles in the daily life of families. An emerging consensus among

---

[8]Francis L. K. Hsu, "Roots of the American Family: From Noah to Now," in Allan J. Lichtman and Joan R. Challinor, eds., *Kin and Communities: Families in America* (Washington, D.C.: Smithsonian Institution Press, 1979), pp. 219–36.

[9]Howard P. Chudacoff, "Newlyweds and Family Extension: The First Stage of the Family Cycle in Providence, Rhode Island, 1864–1865 and 1879–1880," in Tamara K. Hareven and Maris A. Vinovskis, eds., *Family and Population in Nineteenth Century America* (Princeton: Princeton University Press, 1978), pp. 179–205.

[10]John Modell and Tamara K. Hareven, "Urbanization and the Malleable Household: An Examination of Boarding and Lodging in American Families," *Journal of Marriage and the Family* 35 (August 1973), pp. 467–79.

[11]Frances E. Kobrin, "The Fall in Household Size and the Rise of the Primary Individual in the United States," *Demography* 13 (February 1976), pp. 127–38; Howard P. Chudacoff and Tamara K. Hareven, "Family Transitions into Old Age," in Hareven, ed., *Transitions: The Family and the Life Course in Historical Perspective* (New York: Academic Press, 1978), pp. 217–43; Daniel Scott Smith, "Life Course, Norms, and the Family System of Older Americans in 1900," *Journal of Family History* 4 (Fall 1979), pp. 285–98.

scholars challenges traditional accounts of the isolated nuclear family, suggesting instead that kinship networks of mutual aid, service, and emotional support have been as typical of the American experience as the nuclear household itself. Despite migration from abroad and mobility within the new land, writes Tamara K. Hareven, "kin networks were gradually reconstituted through chain migration. Kin played an important role in attracting immigrants to a new area, in facilitating settlement and job location, and in providing assistance in critical life situations." Kinship, she argues, proved to be a far more adaptable institution than traditional theory would have led us to believe. Migrants to cities, for instance, adapted patterns of kin support "to the industrial system and developed new functions for kin which were considerably different from those customarily performed in rural society."[12]

An emphasis on kinship relations also reveals that families may not be founded on a primary household residence or the conventionally expected roles of mothers and fathers. In an anthropological study of a poor Black community, conducted during the 1960s, Carol B. Stack found that families were flexible groups united mainly by the need for mutual aid in the face of scarce resources and recurrent crises. Cooperating kin groups of both relatives and fictive kin—friends who assumed the rights and obligations of blood kin—shared the rearing of children and other domestic tasks. Parental roles were not necessarily assumed by biological mothers and fathers, but by various members of the kin group at different times. One family member might be in charge of discipline, another in charge of curing illness, and yet another in charge of education.[13] Although little is known about such cooperating kin groups in past time, it is clear that key participants in family life may be invisible to those who fail to recognize the malleability of conventional family roles.

Finally, the historical predominance of the nuclear household has not precluded change in other key elements of household structure. Despite enhanced longevity, decreasing fertility has reduced the proportion of households with more than two or three children. (Except for the baby boom of the late 1940s and 1950s, fertility rates have steadily decreased in America since 1800.) According to census returns, the percentage of five- and six-person households has dropped from 27 percent at the time of the first census in 1790 to 14 percent in 1970. During the same period, the percentage of households with seven or more persons has plummeted from 36 percent to just four percent. In the words of Peter Uhlenberg, this change in family life "has radically reduced the number of persons with more than three siblings, has reduced structural change in the family during childhood, and has sharply increased the number who have a low birth order position. As the number of children per mother has declined, the variability in age of parents was reduced. The social, psychological, and economic consequences of these

---
[12]Tamara K. Hareven, "Modernization and Family History: Perspectives on Social Change," *Signs: Journal of Women in Culture and Society* 2 (Autumn 1976), p. 196.
[13]Carol B. Stack, *All Our Kin* (New York: Harper and Row, 1974).

major structural changes in childhood experiences have received almost no attention."[14]

The twentieth century has also witnessed a sharp climb in the proportion of households containing just one or two persons. Between 1900 and 1973, the percentage of one-person households rose from five percent to 19 percent. The rise of households shared by two persons occurred mainly between 1900 and 1950, as life expectancy soared and couples had their last child at increasingly earlier ages. The "empty nest" of parents with departed children, David H. Fischer suggests, is primarily a phenomenon of the twentieth century: "Early in the nineteenth century, parents began to live beyond the period of their children's dependency. In 1850, they did so only by a year or two on the average. But by 1950 the last child was grown and gone from the home when most parents were still in their forties—and still in the full vigor of adult life. A new period of life had come into being: that between adulthood and old age."[15]

Most of the growth in one-person households has taken place since 1950 and resulted from unmarried children leaving home at earlier ages, as well as from the combination of an increased proportion of widows in the population and their greater propensity than before to form separate households. According to Frances E. Kobrin, this "great increase in persons living separately from families, and the concentration of these people at the youngest and oldest stages of the adult life cycle, indicate two major changes: that a process of age-segregation is going on, and that there is a decreasing tolerance for family forms which include non-nuclear members." In contrast to scholars who stress links among residentially dispersed kin, Kobrin concludes that changing household structure has produced generations that "are now much less visible to each other" than at any other time in American history.[16]

FAMILY STABILITY

In addition to the alleged shift from extended to nuclear families, historical research has challenged the notion of a once solid family now crumbling under the pressure of modern society. As the golden age of American family life recedes into mythology, the new wisdom is that whereas families are now significantly more likely than in past times to be disrupted voluntarily by divorce, they are significantly less likely to be disrupted involuntarily by death, disease, and economic privation. Reduced mortality and high rates of both marriage (96 percent) and remarriage (79 percent) have also meant that people today are more likely than their counterparts in pre-twentieth century America to complete a full life cycle that includes marriage, child-rearing, and middle and old age.

---

[14]Peter Uhlenberg, "Changing Configurations of the Life Course," in Hareven, ed., *Transitions*, pp. 77–78.
[15]David H. Fischer, *Growing Old in America* (New York: Oxford University Press, 1977), p. 107.
[16]Kobrin, "The Fall in Household Size," p. 79.

Except for a brief period during the post-World War II baby boom, the American divorce rate has steadily increased since the late nineteenth century. An estimated 38 percent of all marriages taking place during the mid-1970s will end in divorce (compared with less than five percent for marriages of the 1870s). Although 79 percent of divorced Americans currently remarry, contrary to popular lore, the probability of divorce is even higher for a second marriage (44 percent) than for a first marriage. Largely as a consequence of divorce, about four out of every ten children born during the 1970s will spend time in a household headed by a single parent—usually the mother, despite the women's movement and changing divorce laws.

The low incidence of divorce in colonial and nineteenth-century America did not mean, however, that children invariably grew to maturity with the same parents present, or that couples rarely separated until old age. In earlier times, death was far more likely than it is today to claim parents during the childrearing years. In the United States, a dramatic decline in death rates has occurred since 1900, outstripping the total mortality decline of all prior years of American history. In an ingenious essay on "Death and the Family," Uhlenberg found that, given the mortality levels "characteristic of 1900," about 24 percent of all children could expect to lose at least one parent before reaching age 15. For the mortality levels of 1976, the percentage falls to only five percent. Children were far more likely to be orphaned in the past—one child in 62 could expect to lose both parents according to the 1900 mortality rates, as compared to only one child in 1,800 under the mortality characteristic of 1976. Under 1900 mortality conditions, moreover, only one-fourth of all children could expect to have all four grandparents alive at the time of their birth, as compared to two-thirds of today's children.[17]

The elevated mortality of earlier years also translates into a high frequency of marriages that were broken by death prior to old age. According to Uhlenberg's estimates, turn-of-the-century mortality conditions yielded a 67 percent probability that one or both marriage partners would die within 40 years of their marriage (assuming that the groom was age 25 and the bride was age 22). Today, that probability has declined to 36 percent, more than offsetting the corresponding rise in divorce. For Americans marrying in the mid-1970s, the probability is greater than in colonial or nineteenth-century America that the wife and husband will still be together after forty years. This probability is now 40 percent, compared to 29 percent for divorce and mortality rates prevailing in 1900.[18]

Children in past times were also much more likely than today to experience the deaths of siblings. When the death of children is included in mortality calculations, the probability of a child losing either a sibling or a parent is 51 percent for the mortality rates of 1900, but only nine percent for the mortality rates of 1976. These calculations do not take into account the

---
[17]Peter Uhlenberg, "Death and the Family," *Journal of Family History* 5 (Fall 1980), pp. 315–16.
[18]*Ibid.*, p. 317.

declining number of children born to twentieth-century mothers. Far more than in the past, children are now removed from the immediate experience of death within the nuclear family.[19]

Families of the nineteenth and early twentieth century, living in an era of comparatively low wages and little job security and lacking the protection of either private insurance or government assistance, also faced greater economic variability and risk than do families of today. Greater economic uncertainty in the earlier period, Modell persuasively argues, induced "defensive" modes of cooperation within the nuclear family and introduced unplanned variations in family life "not reflected in ideal statements about modal families under average conditions." Modell questions the supposition that modernization has undermined the traditional form of the "ideal" family and thus led to greater variation and spontaneity within families. He suggests, instead, that declining uncertainty in the twentieth century has actually "led to diminished variety in family life."[20]

Further widening the gap between "ideal" and "real" families of past times is the recent finding that people growing up in the nineteenth century followed a less regular and predictable path through stages of childhood and adulthood than they do today. Although biographers thrive on the unique episodes of particular lives, life-course analysis, as pioneered by social scientists such as Reuben Hill and Glen Elder, suggests that superimposed on individual biographies are common phases of life history marked by definite points of exit and entry. According to Elder, "An individual's life course is multi-dimensional since movement through successive life stages entails the concurrent assumption of multiple roles, from those of son or daughter, age-mate, and student during years of dependency to adult lives of activity in major institutional domains of society."[21] Studies of the life course indicate, for instance, that most American males of the nineteenth and twentieth centuries passed through the same transitions of leaving the parental home, marrying, having children, completing some years of education, and entering the workforce. Yet, the timing of the sequence and duration of the transitions seem to have become more regular and predictable over the years. As Modell, Furstenburg, and Hershberg explain, "the broad latitude of choice that characterized growing up in the nineteenth century has been replaced today by a more prescribed and tightly defined schedule of life-course organization."[22] In the colonial period and nineteenth century, the stages of life that we now recognize as infancy, childhood, young adulthood, middle-age, and old-age were much less sharply defined than they are today.

---

[19] *Ibid.*, p. 315.
[20] John Modell, "Changing Risks, Changing Adaptations: American Families in the Nineteenth and Twentieth Centuries," in Lichtman and Challinor, eds., *Kin and Communities*, pp. 119–44.
[21] Glen H. Elder, Jr., "Family History and the Life Course," in Hareven, ed., *Transitions*, p. 26.
[22] John Modell, Frank F. Furstenburg, Jr., and Theodore Hershberg, "Social Change and Transitions to Adulthood in Historical Perspective," *Journal of Family History* 2 (Autumn 1976), p. 28.

THE FAMILY AND THE WORLD OUTSIDE

The traditional model of American family history may come nearest to the mark in its description of changing relations between the family and the external world. The development of a capitalist, industrial order in the United States segregated work physically and psychologically from the home. And the rise of helping professions and the welfare state has, indeed, stripped the family of functions that it once performed. The full implications of these profound changes have yet to be explored.

During the past century and a half, the United States has evolved from a nation of self-sufficient farmers, artisans, and shopkeepers to a nation in which most citizens labor for wages and salaries in enterprises which they do not own. This occupational shift has not only removed the workplace from the home, but has also created two culturally distinct spheres of life. The sphere of work and commerce is marked by the pursuit of self-interest, the rational calculation of gains and losses, competition with peers, and the subordination of ends to means. A worker's time is not his or her own but is sold to employers at the prevailing rate of exchange. To advance into higher levels of status and compensation, workers must compete against others seeking the same positions. The family sphere, in contrast, is marked by solidarity and cooperation among kin, by love and intimacy, by activities that are ends in themselves, and by an orientation toward the fulfillment of tasks and the satisfaction of needs, rather than the budgeting and selling of time.

During the nineteenth century, the two spheres of work and the family came to be differentiated by sex. Despite the frequent dependence of families on multiple wages, nineteenth-century ideology squarely placed responsibility for a family's economic welfare on the male "family head." This responsibility created a moral obligation to labor which transcended any purely instrumental calculation of costs and benefits. It also provided a material basis for male authority within the home and cordoned the world of enterprise as an exclusively male preserve. The home, in turn, was the proper place for the "true woman," whose cardinal virtues of piety, purity, submissiveness, and domesticity assured the proper rearing of children and the necessary support and comfort for hard-working husbands. On woman's shoulders was placed the weighty responsibility of preserving the stability of the Republic by rearing its future citizens and preventing its menfolk from succumbing to lust and dissipation. "The woman's magazines and related literature," wrote Barbara Welter, "sought to convince woman that she had the best of both worlds—power and virtue—and that a stable order of society depended upon her maintaining her traditional place in it."[23] Thus, those with a stake in the status quo used fears of an eroding family to keep women in their place and resist social change.

[23]Barbara Welter, "The Cult of True Womanhood: 1820–1860," *American Quarterly* 18 (Summer 1966), p. 168.

In our own times, this ideology of separate spheres for males and females has apparently survived both the women's movement and a remarkable change in the actual division of labor according to sex. Between 1900 and 1976, the proportion of women working outside the home soared from about 20 to 56 percent. Women now constitute more than 40 percent of the American labor force, and the federal government has officially endorsed the goals of ending employment discrimination by sex and assuring equal pay for equal work. Yet, males continue to command the best jobs and gain substantially higher compensation than their female counterparts. According to recent surveys, most women still consider the rearing of children, rather than the pursuit of a career, as their primary responsibility.

An insightful analysis of work roles by Steven Dubnoff indicates that the current situation meets the needs of a capitalist economy without upsetting the balance of power within the family. "Late capitalism," he wrote, "requires both a supply of well-motivated primary workers and a supply of ill-paid secondary workers. . . . The increasing labor-force participation of women in the post-war era provided a supply of such secondary workers, maintained consumption in a period of declining real wages, and does not seem to affect materially the division of labor and functions within the family."[24]

One of the most notable trends in the modernization of American society is the assumption of responsibility for family welfare and education by organizations outside the family. Since the era of the American Revolution, families have become increasingly dependent upon the judgment and authority of experts such as doctors, lawyers, and social workers. The forms of practice within such helping professions now have profound implications for the lives of family members. In the twentieth century, families have come to be dependent on such government programs as food stamps, social security, medicare, and aid to families with dependent children. Families have become ever more reliant on the services of institutions such as hospitals, asylums, and old-age homes.

Scholars are just beginning to probe the precise timing and consequences of these changes. In a study of nineteenth-century Massachusetts, for instance, Barbara G. Rosenkrantz and Maris A. Vinovskis disclose a mid-century shift away from family care for the insane as government assumed financial responsibility for the insane and established asylums for their treatment. Asylums, they note, were originally founded by optimistic, humane reformers intent upon offering the best available therapy to the mentally ill. For the government supporting these asylums, however, the goals of controlling costs and incarcerating those deemed dangerous to society displaced the goal of treating the insane. The reformers themselves found that curing the insane was far more difficult than they had initially anticipated. By the late nineteenth century, the asylum had been transformed from a

---

[24]Steven Dubnoff, "Gender, the Family, and the Problem of Work Motivation in a Transition to Industrial Capitalism," *Journal of Family History* 4 (Summer 1979), p. 134.

place of refuge and therapy into an institution for the cheap custody of people forgotten and ignored by the rest of society.[25]

The external world also intrudes on the family in the basic sense that individuals and family groups live out their lives in different historical circumstances. As Anne Foner correctly observes, historians must pay attention to differences among cohorts of families—"aggregates of familes who start family life in the same period and proceed through the family cycle together. . . . Just as the individual is a product of his times, so is the family affected by its cohort membership and by the social and economic conditions of the period through which it passes."[26] Equally important are variations in the experiences of families within the same cohort. In his study of families during the Great Depression of the 1930s, Elder distinguishes between those families that experienced economic distress and those that did not. Economic deprivation, he discovered, tended to shift economic responsibilities to mothers and older children, to reduce parental control, to diminish the appeal of the father as a role model, and to increase emotional stress. In response to these strains, the sons and daughters of deprived families developed in their adult life an especially strong commitment to traditional sex roles—the mother as parent and homemaker, the father as breadwinner.[27]

Finally, scholars of the family remind us that relations between the family and the outside world are always reciprocal; for the family is not a weather vane buffeted by the winds of change, but an active agent in the making of history. For instance, decisions about childbearing made individually by millions of families may significantly change the conditions of society for the next generation. That generation, in turn, is influenced in its family-planning decisions by the very conditions created by the choices of its forebears. According to Richard A. Easterlin, there is superimposed on the long-term decline in American fertility rates an independent, cyclical pattern of boom and bust in childbearing and economic opportunity. People tend to marry early and begin families, he states, when economic prospects seem good relative to the economic circumstances of the families in which they were raised. In contrast, individuals postpone marriage and childbearing when their earnings prospects appear grim relative to the living standards to which they are accustomed. Thus, young adults produced a baby boom in the late 1940s and 1950s because their economic futures appeared bright, especially in contrast to the experiences of their depression-era parents. However, the children of the baby boom glutted the labor markets of the 1960s and 1970s, dimming their economic prospects and reducing their propensity to marry early and have children. The wheel should turn again, Easterlin contends,

---

[25]Barbara G. Rosenkrantz and Maris A. Vinovskis, "Caring for the Insane in Ante-Bellum Massachusetts: Family, Community, and State Participation," in Lichtman and Challinor, eds., *Kin and Communities*, pp. 187–218.
[26]Anne Foner, "Age Stratification and the Changing Family," in John Demos and Sarane Spence Boocock, eds., *Turning Points: Historical and Sociological Essays on the Family* (Chicago: University of Chicago Press, 1978), p. 358.
[27]Glen H. Elder, Jr., *Children of the Great Depression* (Chicago: University of Chicago Press, 1974).

producing a new baby boom, when the shrunken cohort of the late 1960s and 1970s finds ample opportunity as it comes of age.[28]

CONCLUSION

American family history is still a field in its infancy; much has been learned, but much more remains to be done. Although we know a great deal about matters such as household size and composition that can be documented statistically, historians have yet to probe deeply into the inner workings of the family or to recover the emotional content of family life in past times. Scholars are just beginning to explore differences in the experiences of families from distinct economic classes, ethnic backgrounds, and places of residence. As yet, no general synthesis of American family history has emerged to replace the elegant, if flawed, model set forth in traditional sociology. Recent themes such as the family cycle or life-course analysis are scaffoldings for description, rather than explanatory models of historical change.

American family history is coming of age as a discipline precisely at a time when millions of Americans are affirming the importance of family heritage by seeking to find their own roots in the past. Personal family history, many Americans are coming to recognize, is a unifying theme that transcends the limitations of a single life and offers an enriched sense of identity. By continuing to explore our common family heritage and making new efforts to communicate their findings to a broad audience, historians can contribute answers to the fundamental human questions of who we are, where we came from, how we came to be as we are, and how we differ from those who lived before us.

BIBLIOGRAPHY

Much of the important scholarship in American family history is in article form, rather than book form. Several useful collections of articles are included in the list below. Readers may also wish to consult journals in which work on American family history frequently appears: *Journal of Family History, Journal of Interdisciplinary History, Journal of Social History, Journal of Marriage and the Family, Signs, American Sociological Review,* and *The American Journal of Sociology.*

Degler, Carl N. *At Odds: Women and the Family in America from the Revolution to the Present.* New York: Oxford University Press, 1980. An ambitious, if not entirely convincing, survey of family and women's history and the connections between them.

---

[28]Richard A. Easterlin, *Birth and Fortune: The Impact of Numbers on Personal Welfare* (New York: Basic Books, 1980).

Demos, John. *A Little Commonwealth: Family Life in Plymouth Colony.* New York: Oxford University Press, 1970. A pioneering work that combines psychological theory with research into literary and statistical sources.

Demos, John and Sarane Spence Boocock. *Turning Points: Historical and Sociological Essays on the Family.* Chicago: University of Chicago Press, 1978. Essays from a special supplement of *The American Journal of Sociology.*

Easterlin, Richard A. *Birth and Fortune: The Impact of Numbers on Personal Welfare.* New York: Basic Books, 1980. Sets forth Easterlin's theory of the relationship between fertility and economic opportunity and the quality of life within society.

Elder, Glen H. *Children of the Great Depression: Social Change in Life Experience.* Chicago: University of Chicago Press, 1974. A seminal study of how economic depression affected the family life of those growing up in the 1930s.

Fischer, David H. *Growing Old in America.* New York: Oxford University Press, 1977. An imaginative, if controversial, history of old age in America, from colonial times to the 1970s.

Gordon, Michael, ed. *The American Family in Social-Historical Perspective.* 2nd ed. New York: St. Martin's Press, 1978. A wide-ranging collection of essays that constitutes the best single introduction to American family history.

Greven, Philip J., Jr. *Four Generations: Population, Land, and Family in Colonial Andover, Massachusetts.* Ithaca: Cornell University Press, 1970. A demographic study that links family life to social and economic history.

Gutman, Herbert G., Jr. *The Black Family in Slavery and Freedom 1750–1925.* New York: Pantheon Books, 1976. The key work on the Black family, it challenges the notion that slavery destroyed Black family life.

Hareven, Tamara K., ed. *Transitions: The Family and the Life Course in Historical Perspective.* New York: Academic Press, 1978. A useful introduction to the new field of life-course analysis.

Hareven, Tamara K. and Maris A. Vinovskis, eds. *Family and Population in Nineteenth Century America.* Princeton: Princeton University Press, 1978. Heavily quantitative articles covering themes such as fertility, migration, family structure, and familial economic arrangements.

Lichtman, Allan J. *Your Family History: How to Use Oral History, Personal Family Archives, and Public Documents to Discover Your Heritage.* New York: Random House, 1978. An attempt to integrate insights into family history with guidelines on how to discover one's own heritage. Designed for classroom use.

Lichtman, Allan J. and Joan R. Challinor, eds. *Kin and Communities: Families in America.* Washington, D.C.: Smithsonian Institution Press, 1979. Selections of material from the Smithsonian Institution's Sixth International Symposium on Kin and Communities. Takes a multidisciplinary approach to family history and seeks to communicate to a nontechnical audience.

Rabb, Theodore K. and Robert I. Rotberg, eds. *The Family in History: Interdisciplinary Essays.* New York: Harper and Row, 1971. An important collection of early scholarship in family history drawn primarily from a special issue of the *Journal of Interdisciplinary History.*

Russo, David J. *Families and Communities: A New View of American History.* Nashville: American Association for State and Local History, 1974. Explores possibilities for revising American history through an emphasis on families and localities.

Seward, Rudy Ray. *The American Family: A Demographic History.* Beverly Hills: Sage Publications, 1978. Includes summaries of research on family demography, along with the author's own analysis of census returns from 1850 to 1880. Takes the view that there has been relatively little change in American family structure.

Stack, Carol B. *All Our Kin.* New York: Harper and Row, 1974. Shows that family life may be founded neither on the household nor on conventional notions of kinship roles.

Vinovskis, Maris A. *Studies in American Historical Demography.* New York: Academic Press, 1979. A good introduction to the demographic history of American families; particularly strong on the colonial period.

Wells, Robert V. *The Population of the British Colonies in America Before 1776: A Survey of Census Data.* Princeton: Princeton University Press, 1975. A useful compendium of statistical information that goes beyond the usual focus on the New England colonies.

SUGGESTIONS FOR TEACHING FAMILY HISTORY

Doing Family History Projects with High School Students

G. GALIN BERRIER

The "new social history" is indeed new; so new, in fact, that any social studies teacher who graduated from college as recently as ten years ago could not have read any of the books or articles in Allan J. Lichtman's bibliography in an undergraduate course. It is equally unlikely that much of this recent scholarship will have found its way into current high-school history texts. The teacher wishing to introduce his or her students to this exciting new kind of history will find few signposts to point the way. It can be done through family history projects.

Good family history projects do not just happen. Even the most energetic students need guidance about the kinds of questions to ask. Listed below are some that my own students have found helpful in researching their own families' histories; these questions can also be used to test and reinforce the insights summarized by Lichtman. The teacher might use these questions either to help individual students guide their research on family history projects, or to assist entire classes in a comparative study. In either case, the teacher new to this kind of social history is likely to be pleasantly surprised at the excitement and enthusiasm which family history projects can generate to reinvigorate history teaching.

FAMILY STRUCTURE

How many generations lived at home in your family? In your parents' family? In your grandparents' family?

How much influence, if any, did your grandparents have on your parents' choice of an occupation? Of a marriage partner?

Did your parents ever live in someone else's household? In a household that included boarders? Were there relatives other than children in that household? Were there friends, servants, or other unrelated persons? Ask the same questions of your grandparents.

Did other relatives play a role in helping your parents to settle here? To find a job? To find a place to live? Ask the same questions of your grandparents.

Did anyone other than your grandparents perform the responsibilities of raising your parents? Who was responsible for discipline? For caring for someone who was sick? For helping with school work?

How many brothers and sisters did your parents have? How many did your grandparents have? Did they live in houses, or apartments? Did family members other than parents and children live in the same household? In the same building? Along the same street? In the same neighborhood or community?

Do your grandparents live with you? Near you, or far away? In their own dwellings, or in retirement homes?

FAMILY STABILITY

How many of your grandparents were alive when you were born? Ask the same question of your parents. Of your grandparents. How long were your grandparents married?

Did the age of marriage and the average family size remain stable over time, or did they change? How were pregnancies spaced over time? Was parenthood planned?

How were babies treated? Up to what age was a child regarded as a "child"? Was "adolescence" recognized as a special stage of life? At what age were young people expected to assume adult responsibilities? Was the age the same for sons and daughters?

Did any of your parents' brothers or sisters die before reaching adulthood? Did any of your grandparents' brothers or sisters? What was the family's attitude toward its aged members?

At what age did your parents leave home? Marry? Have their first child? Finish school? Get their first job? Ask the same questions of your grandparents.

THE FAMILY AND THE WORLD OUTSIDE

Does your mother work outside the home? Did (or do) either of your grandmothers?

Did parents help children get started in school? In business, a trade, or a profession? Did sons tend to follow their fathers' occupations? Did grandparents influence the occupational choices of their grandchildren?

What criteria and priorities did the family assign for "success"? (Making a lot of money, having a high status occupation, living in a big house or nice neighborhood, marrying well, getting a college education?)

It is hardly necessary to add that students should be cautioned to use tact when their questions take them into areas of family conflict, or where there are "skeletons" in the family closet. They should also be encouraged to be selective when asking questions. It is not necessary for every family to respond to every single question.

The Family in American Literature

CATHERINE W. EDWARDS

The new research concerning the American family in various historical periods may be presented in the classroom through the use of literature. In contrast to historical documents and statistics, literature provides a more personal interpretation of the fears and hopes of families. Through literature, students also may gain a better understanding of the physical and social forces which affect the security of the family. For students to assess change and stability in American family life, it is essential for them to use several pieces of literature from various times in American history. The three pieces suggested below were selected for their literary quality, subject matter, readability, and availability to the secondary school teacher. Each of the recommended activities should be preceded by a background lecture or student activities dealing with the community structure and living conditions found in the specific location and historical period of each piece of literature.

COLONIAL FAMILY
Students will:
1. Read three poems by Anne Bradstreet: "Before the Birth of One of Her Children," "In Memory of My Dear Grandchild Elizabeth Bradstreet, Who Deceased August, 1665," and "Upon the Burning of Our House, July 10, 1666." They are included in Ann Stanford, *The Women Poets in English: An Anthology* (New York: McGraw-Hill, 1972).
2. Discuss the following questions as they relate to the Bradstreet poems and the colonial period in general: What creates instability in the colonial family? Why is Bradstreet preoccupied with death? What gives Bradstreet hope when she is confronted with disaster? What kind of economic security do the Bradstreets have?
3. Using a narrative form, write a separate journal entry describing the events of each poem.

FARMING/IMMIGRANT FAMILY
Students will:
1. Read Willa Cather's *My Antonia* (Boston: Houghton Mifflin, 1918).
2. Discuss the following questions: Why does Antonia's family immigrate to the United States? Why does Antonia's father commit suicide? How does the family respond? What kinds of upward mobility do the Burdens and the Shimerdas experience? Describe Antonia's lifestyle when Jim returns for a visit? Does the reader expect a different ending? If so, why?
3. Write a letter dated ten years after Jim and Antonia's last meeting. The letter should be written by either Jim or Antonia and describe his or her family life and the events that have occurred in the past ten years. Before writing, students should think about the goals of the author of the letter.

SUBURBAN FAMILY
Students will:
1. Read orally Arthur Miller's *Death of a Salesman* (New York: Viking Press, 1949). (This should take two to three class periods, depending on the reading skills of the students.)
2. Discuss the following questions: How do the characters reflect values in America after World War II? Describe the goals of each of the main characters. Describe the goals of the family as a unit. Why does Willy commit suicide? How is isolation portrayed in the play? Are there other forms of death besides physical death? What are they? How does community and physical mobility affect the characters in the play?
3. Write two epitaphs for Willy. First, write from his point of view; then write from your own point of view.

COMPARATIVE APPROACH

In order to compare the structure and stability of American families in various historical periods, the teacher may want to have the students draw conclusions based on the literature they have read. The following questions may guide the students' generalizations: What has security meant to families in different periods of American history? How does economic uncertainty affect the family? In what ways are families isolated in American society? How does physical and economic mobility affect the family? How is the stability of the family shaken in different historical periods? What has replaced death as a major agent of change within the family in the twentieth century?

RESEARCH PROJECTS

In order to increase their understanding, students may:
1. Develop charts and graphs comparing the increase of divorce to the decline of death within family units. Peter Uhlenberg, "Death and the Family," *Journal of Family History* 5 (Fall 1980): 313-320.
2. Create maps of typical community groupings in colonial, farming, and suburban American societies.

Teaching Family History Using Museum and Community Resources

PETER S. O'CONNELL

Teachers interested in using the new family history materials and methods have met with some difficulties. Whereas students experience contemporary family life in an active, personal way—often with some conflict—family history is presented by historians in an abstract and formal way; students may not often connect their personal experiences with those of families in the past. The teacher who starts out to find family history materials and bring them to life faces an enormous task. Few teachers have the time, even if they possess the skills. Student family histories and oral history approaches get the class back to 1900, but what about the nineteenth century? How can a teacher capitalize on the excitement engendered by local community resources without losing track of the broader picture?

At Old Sturbridge Village in Sturbridge, Massachusetts, we have developed packets of primary resources, family role cards, and a teaching sequence that ask students to compare family life in the present with family life in New England around 1830. The approach involves the selection of a *sample* of primary resources on the basis of existing published research, the inclusion of available local materials, and a field study of a local historic house or outdoor history museum.

THE FAMILY IN AMERICAN HISTORY

Using published family history sources to establish regional family norms (age of marriage, family size, infant death, the inclusion of non-nuclear members in the household), a teacher uses *local* census material and vital records to select a sample of a dozen families that together are representative of the norms. Using the bibliography from published sources, the teacher identifies key source materials and then edits, reproduces, and organizes them by topics appropriate to family history (childhood, education, courtship, attitudes toward discipline, work choice). The process is represented graphically in Figure 1:

Figure 1.

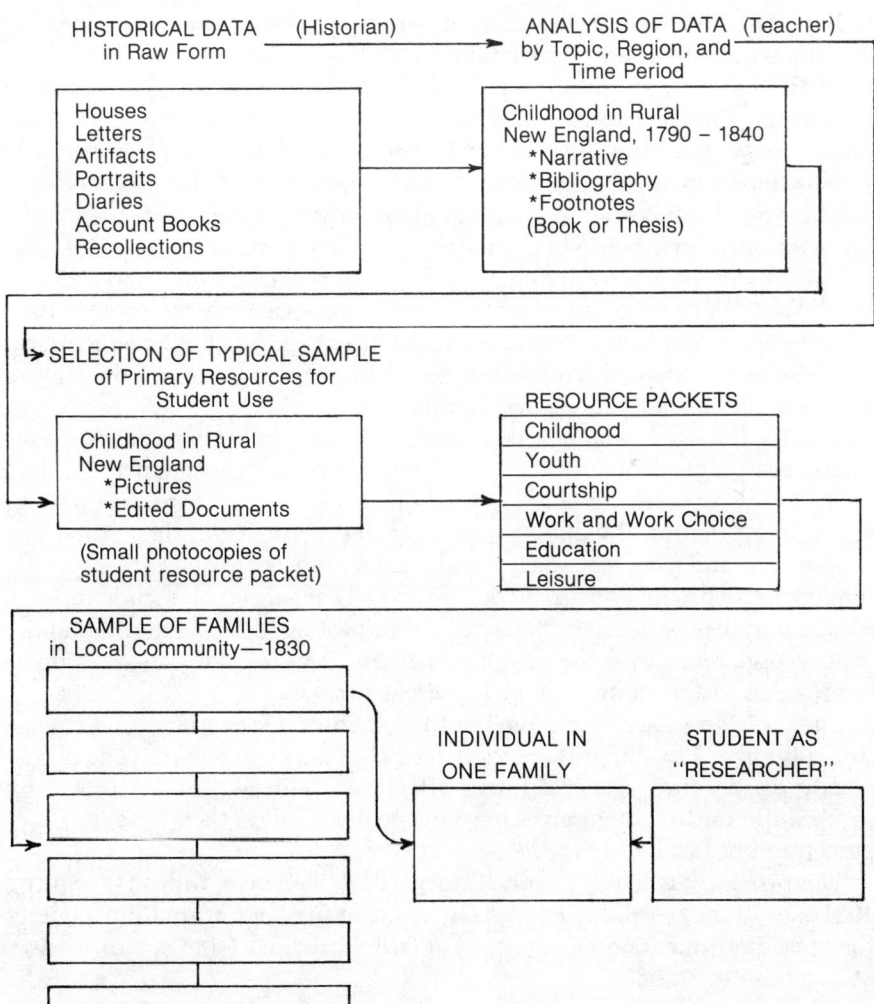

The teaching sequence begins with student family experiences in the present and reverses the direction of the chart. Students are asked to do a census of their own classes, to make inventories of their own houses, to keep diaries of family activities, and to analyze these sources for evidence of patterns. These activities develop a set of skills and familiarity with *types* of historical documents. The patterns are compared with norms for the population as a whole, developing the concept of a *sample*.

Students are then ready to begin their historical inquiry. Each student is assigned an identity of a member of a family in the 1830s to investigate. (Old Sturbridge Village has developed a *sample* of thirty-five households and families representative of norms for the 320 families living in Sturbridge in 1830. Teachers can use these or develop their own sample using their town's vital statistics and census.) The students make tentative conclusions about family norms from their class sample, and they raise questions they need to investigate if they are to understand more fully family life in 1830.

With these questions in mind, students read primary sources (Old Sturbridge Village resources are organized by stages of life cycle—childhood, youth, courtship, aging—or by topic—work choice, pleasure, farm life) taken from regional collections and supplemented by any available primary materials pertaining to the students' town. The students then visit a museum or historic house to gather evidence from artifacts and to imagine themselves more clearly living in a particular place, time, and cultural context. Students are often asked to role-play a decision on a particular issue (whether to go to a factory town, to the West, or to pursue higher education), as a way of analyzing the impact of general historical trends on the choices and activities of individuals and families.

In class discussion, students compare and contrast family patterns, arrive at patterns typical of most families, and develop hypotheses to explain differences in experiences as a result of family wealth, structure, occupation, education, or cultural values. Students read excerpts from their American history texts and from secondary family history sources to place their specific inquiry into a broader historical perspective. Teachers involve students in an ideal research experience with few of the stumbling blocks of normal family history research. Once this is done in depth, the teacher can use similar approaches in the study of later historical periods.

The basic approach works well with elementary, secondary, and college students alike. The students are excited by the chance to research one family and to discuss more general forces affecting family life in the 1830s. By successfully putting themselves in someone else's shoes, they have a clearer perception of family life in the present.

This process of teaching family history is described more fully in the Spring 1981 issue of the *Journal of Family History*. For further information, contact the Museum Education Department at Old Sturbridge Village, Sturbridge, Massachusetts 01566.

The Black Family in American History: A Classroom Lesson

THOMAS L. DYNNESON

This lesson was developed for teachers who would like to have their students examine some of the problems of Black family life. The Black family is especially appropriate for this purpose because it has had to overcome slavery, which was especially threatening to the development of marriage, childrearing, and family living. The lesson consists of a teachers' scenario, two case studies, and a list of suggested discussion items for the classroom. The case studies describe two fictional Black families that might have existed at the time of slavery and during the height of migration to Northern industrial cities. The teacher is encouraged to have the students compare these Black families with each other and with non-Black families of the same era. The discussion items are included as suggested topics for classroom use.

TEACHERS' SCENARIO

The Black family has had to survive the ordeals of slavery, economic poverty, and social discrimination, which have combined to weaken the bonds of family stability. No other group has had to overcome so many obstacles to develop stable kinship and family ties. Although the slaves maintained a form of family life, it had no legal existence. While many free Black families did exist in the South, as well as in the North, prior to emancipation, the overwhelming majority of Blacks lived in quasi-family situations in the South. After the Civil War, the bulk of the Black population remained in the South as sharecroppers and tenant farmers. The rural Black family experienced the poverty that swept the South after emancipation. The only escape from rural poverty was migration to Northern cities. Migration of Blacks lured to Northern industrial cities by jobs and higher wages during World War I also weakened the bonds of family living. When job opportunities diminished in the Northern cities, these Black families faced problems different from those of families who chose to stay in the rural South.

CASE STUDY: THE SLAVE FAMILY

Cato and Sophia were born as slaves on the Rutlege plantation. After four generations, the Rutlege family had built its plantation into a successful and prosperous operation. Two hundred field slaves and eight house servants provided the labor and services.

Cato had been born to Tess, and Sophia to Rachael two years later. For most of her life, Sophia took care of the younger slave children while their mothers worked in the fields. Cato had worked as a field hand since he was twelve. At the age of sixteen, he drove a team of mules. In the evenings, the mothers and fathers returned to their cabins to tend to their own chores and to take care of their children. In 1810, a financial crisis had forced the Rutlege family to sell twenty male field hands. Cato's father was one of the twenty. He would never return to the Rutlege Plantation. Even though Cato was considered the man in the family, his mother ruled the cabin and was both mother and father to the children.

When Sophia became eighteen, Cato wanted to marry her. One evening, Rachael went to the mansion and asked to see Betty, Mrs. Rutlege's personal maid. Rachael asked Betty to talk to Mrs. Rutlege about the marriage of Cato and Sophia. A week later, Betty sent for Rachael and informed her that Cato and Sophia would be given materials to build a cabin. After the cabin was built, Ambros, the slave preacher, married the two by reciting some memorized phrases from the Bible. Mrs. Rutlege and her daughter came down that evening with some extra rations and items for the new cabin. Everything that the master and slaves needed came from the plantation.

For over thirty years, Cato and Sophia lived in that same cabin. Cato's mother, Tess, lived with them in her old age. Cato and Sophia had ten children, six of whom continued to live as adults on the Rutlege Plantation in their own cabins.

CASE STUDY: THE URBAN FAMILY IN 1918

Rose Brown left her family in Mississippi in order to find work in Chicago. Rose was the third of nine children born to tenant farmers. Their farm consisted of forty acres, a team of mules, and a five-room shanty. Each year one-third of the cotton crop raised on the farm went to pay the landowner. Rose's relatives lived in the same area and they visited after church on Sunday. Rose's cousin had left Mississippi the year before and had found work in Chicago. Rose had heard about the jobs and wages in the North, so she decided to leave her parents and brothers and sisters.

After arriving in Chicago, she was met by her cousin and went to live with her until she could find work and a place of her own. Jobs were plentiful because of the war in Europe. Rose found that she could not find a job in the factories where the wages were high. They wanted only men. She did find work as a cleaning lady in one of the older hotels in the city. Rose earned her own money for the first time.

One day, Rose met Frederick Godsey, a man from Alabama who had moved North to find work. Six months later they were married. They rented a five-room apartment on the South Side of Chicago. For six years, things were good. Frederick had a job in the foundry, and four children were born. The oldest boy was William Godsey. Conditions became very difficult for the Godsey family when Frederick lost his job due to a slowdown at the foundry. Soon the Godsey family had to move to a smaller apartment, and Rose had to go back to work. After a year, with only temporary jobs, Frederick left the family and never returned again. One day, William and three of his friends were arrested for taking money from a neighborhood store. They were sent to a correctional school for juveniles. Later, William would leave the family for a life in the streets. Rose continued to work in order to support her children. She found kinship with her friends in the church, and her other children stayed with her until they married and started their own families.

SUGGESTED CLASSROOM TOPICS

The following items are recommended as classroom discussion topics that may be helpful in clarifying the issues that are raised in the case studies.
- The role and function of family members in the operation of the family.
- The effects of slavery on Black fathers and mothers in terms of their roles in the family.
- The need for legal protection of the family (something that was not granted to the slave family).
- Childrearing practices and problems of both the slave and urban families.
- Courtship and marriage as part of the slave family.
- The economic function of the family.
- The family as a support system for children and newly married couples.
- The issues of authority in the family. Decision-making processes and the effect of an absence of authority.
- The role of the family in preventing juvenile delinquency and crime in the community.
- Making comparisons of Black family life with non-Black families of the same period.
- Similarities of today's families with the slave and urban families of the past. Consider the high divorce rate and the working mother of today.

REFERENCES

Bracey, John H., Jr., August Meier, and Elliot Rudwick. *Black Matriarchy: Myth or Reality*. Belmont, Calif: Wadsworth Publishing Co., 1971.

Du Bois, W.E.B. *The Negro American Family*. Cambridge, Mass: The M.I.T. Press, 1970.

Frazier, E. Franklin. *The Negro in the United States*. Chicago: The University of Chicago Press, 1948.

Gutman, Herbert G. *The Black Family in Slavery and Freedom, 1750–1925*. New York: Pantheon Books, 1976.

Heiss, Jerold. *The Case of the Black Family: A Sociological Inquiry*. New York: Columbia University Press, 1975.

McCord, William, et al. *Life Styles in the Black Ghetto*. New York: W.W. Norton and Company, Inc., 1969.

Scanzoni, John J. *The Black Family in Modern Society*. Boston: Allyn and Bacon, Inc., 1971.

Sherman, Richard B., ed. *The Negro and the City*. Englewood Cliffs, New Jersey: Prentice-Hall, Inc., 1970.

TEACHING AMERICAN HISTORY: NEW DIRECTIONS

EPA DOCUMERICA PHOTO BY CHARLES O'REAR

CHAPTER 3

Social History and the Teaching of History

PETER N. STEARNS

THE RISE OF social history has been, without question, the most striking development in American historical scholarship over the past two decades. Gertrude Himmelfarb, writing on the general status of American historical research for the *New York Times* book review section, was indeed moved to ask whether virtually all serious history has not become social-historical in bent. Thus, intellectual historians turn to concerns about the spread of ideas and their impact on more popular attitudes and behaviors. Political historians, using quantitative methods, examine the class and ethnic characteristics of electorates and constituencies. Certainly, many of the special topics that catch the eye in recent historical writing—women's history and Black and ethnic history, to use two examples—have moved steadily into the orbit of social history. Consequently, a generation of writings on great women and ideas about women has yielded to primary attention to the activities of more ordinary women in more ordinary phases of life—women's work, health, and family.

FOUR IMPORTANT QUESTIONS

It is not the purpose of this chapter to prove that social history has become *the* dominant approach in American historical scholarship. Indeed, as a social historian, I find it pleasant to disclaim some work as the problem of some other subdiscipline. Nevertheless, the undoubted and continued rise of social history raises four important questions for the teaching of history at virtually all levels, but particularly in the secondary schools:
1. Why has social history not caught on as a teaching approach to the extent that it has pervaded historical research?
2. What is social history?
3. Should social history be more widely taught (the answer is "yes"), and why?
4. How can social history be translated into the classroom?

Question 1 need not detain us very long, although it is an interesting subject. Social history is sufficiently new, despite its rapid gains, that not only many school teachers, but many historians who are still training teachers, are not attuned to it. Without some rather explicit reorientation of interests, the nature of social history (Question 2) complicates its translation into teaching. Social historians, themselves, caught in the excitement of new research topics, have spent more time on scholarship than on dissemination, sometimes writing—even more avidly than most historical scholars usually do—for other academics alone. The slowing of recruitment of new teachers, and the growing sluggishness of new textbook production and purchase add to the difficulties of bridging gaps among various kinds of history teachers. Of course, some social history subjects have penetrated some texts, and some imaginative courses have developed around certain social history topics in some schools. But, generally, the proposition that social history teaching has lagged is accurate, and the reasons are not hard to find.

It must also be noted that the very real difficulties teachers may face in "picking up" a social history orientation are not necessarily faced by students, who have less past training or preconceived notions about history to reconsider. This statement, in turn, leads logically to Question number 4, which Linda Rosenzweig takes up in the next part of this Bulletin, dealing with a major new project to translate key social history approaches and findings into high school curricula.

This leaves us with Questions 2 and 3 as the central concerns of the present chapter. The argument is that social history's position in research scholarship is sufficiently significant that history teachers should at least acquaint themselves with it; that the definition of social history reveals it as something more than a new topic or two, but rather as a distinctive form of history that requires some explicit adjustment by those acquainted with more conventional history (an adjustment that need not be unpleasant); and that there are several compelling reasons for introducing a serious social history component into secondary school history and social studies teaching. This argument leads logically to the next part of this Bulletin, which shows how social history can be taught at the high school level.

THE NATURE OF SOCIAL HISTORY

Social history is, in one sense, easy enough to define. It involves a central focus on the ordinary activities and outlook of ordinary people. The first wave of interest in social history in the United States particularly emphasized the "ordinary people" aspects: social historians wrote histories of groups previously regarded as inarticulate. Hence, social historians probed more deeply into the history of slavery or the labor movement, getting beyond the formal structures of plantation life or trade union politics to basic aspirations and conditions of actual slaves or factory workers. Thus, groups virtually ignored by previous historians—housewives or urban Blacks—became subjects for a rather rich literature.

More recently, social historians have added to the concern for important *groups* a concern for important *activities* outside the mainstream of conventional historical research; for example, research on the history of sexuality, health practices, childbearing, and other areas. Activities are traced in terms of their own dynamics—how past childrearing norms affect more recent patterns—but, above all, in their relationship to the larger human experiences. Changes in sexuality thus link to changes in economic behavior, while nutritional habits affect and are affected by women's roles. Social historians are attempting to complete the historical picture, leaving out no group or facet of individual or social experience. The whole fabric of society has a history, not just selected aspects such as politics or formal intellectual life. This "total history" enriches an understanding of even familiar historical topics; for example, changes in childhood patterns may affect political outlook. It is, or can be, compellingly interesting. And it gives vital historical perspective to activities—sexual behavior is an obvious example—that we know are important, that are, in fact, conditioned by the past, but that we are inclined to consider without serious historical context.

It is important to stress that the basic definition of social history does not involve a distinctive methodology. Social historians often use distinctive sources, but, like other historians, they mix impressionistic evidence with quantitative data in various combinations. It is through topical range and approach that social historians carve the distinctiveness of their field.

Social history thus represents a broadening of the range of historical topics and a reevaluation of priorities in the study of history. Social historians (as may have become obvious by now) are dreadful imperialists. They urge not simply an addition to the list of historical subjects, but a new kind of overall approach to history. Hence, while they argue against an exclusive focus on political developments, they, too, are concerned with main lines of political history: for example, the advent of new political attitudes and behaviors among significant groups of people, or the impact of new state forms or functions on other aspects of life. Similarly, social historians can be almost as interested in the Enlightenment or Romanticism as intellectual historians are, but they approach them in terms less of formal ideological causations than of linkage with developments in society; and they are vitally concerned with *how* and *why* new concepts spread beyond the intellectual orbit. Social historians have not worked out all the links among the various facets of the social experience—which is one reason that their relationship to conventional history remains fuzzy—but their intent to embrace the whole experience is clear enough.

The relative newness of social history goes beyond a longer list of subjects that have histories and a reordering of priorities in the historical record. It includes a distinctive sense of chronology. Social historians are concerned more with processes than with events. They mark time in decades, more than in months or even years. The advent of the modern demographic framework, in which families cut back on the average number of children born, can be perceived only in terms of a decade or two. Social history, of course, deals with events—the impact of war, the causes of revolution—but it inserts them into broader processes; it does not use them as organizing units. This is one example of social historians' somewhat distinctive style, as well as subject matter. It is a style potentially complicated: a less concrete framework for the recording of change. Correspondingly, teachers who move into the field of social history will find a set of problems and pleasures somewhat different from that of strictly conventional political and diplomatic history.

WHY STUDY SOCIAL HISTORY?

Why bother? We have argued that social history is novel, not just in specific subject matter but in approach, and that it cannot be encompassed simply by extending the tools of mainstream political history. This means that the teaching of social history requires some retooling, and that means some effort and discomfort. Why not, given everything else there is to do in a rather gloomy educational climate at present, just stick to the tried and true? It is certainly not as easy now as it was a decade ago to justify innovation for its own sake, or to promise a vast surge of interest in history if just this one new tactic is added. We turn to the issue of justifying some teaching time for social history, an effort clearly needed in our jaded educational climate and one which will also elaborate on the sense of what social history is.

Why study the history of leisure, or of health practices, or of childrearing at the high school level? Why rock a back-to-basics boat by arguing that the basics of history have changed and can be captured only by curriculum innovation?

The most obvious reason—although not the most important—follows from the clear divergence between history scholarship and history teaching since social history's rise. The introduction of a serious social history component into the schools will help to narrow the gap that has opened up between school history, on the one hand, and the research edge of history—and along with it much college-level history teaching—on the other: school history has not changed nearly as much as research history has. Understandably, college curricula have kept up better, which means that there is a wider school/college gap in curriculum emphasis than there once was.

Identifying a gap is, of course, not the same thing as proving that it should be closed. High school teachers and students might well claim special learning needs or socialization needs that keep school history different in content, as well as in level of sophistication, from research history. This is the case already in France, where almost all historical research is in social history—usually at a very high average level—but where school history remains resolutely political and cultural, stressing the political development of France and its intellectual glories. Viewed from afar, this split—which is really a reflection of the French belief, only somewhat modified in recent years, that school education is to inculcate the masses, whereas real intellectual life is reserved for an elite—does not look particularly attractive, at least for an American context. I would question its political implications, and I would certainly question the division in the definition and use of history which it promotes.

But this is only the first step in justifying change; for the next, we must look to the implications of social history for the schools themselves. I have already suggested that certain themes of social history greatly enrich the understanding of conventional history. It is now needlessly narrow, even arid, to approach the revolutionary period of early nineteenth-century Europe (or the urban agitation and Jacksonian democracy of the same period in the United States) without serious attention to the crisis in work values and work settings attendant upon the advent not only of factories but of larger market relationships. The drama of conflicting views—largely traditional on the part of the working classes, and maximization-oriented in the case of the new middle classes—is a vital facet of social history; but it also, obviously, informed the tide of political change and the ambiguous results of political protest. Only a bit less obviously, the results of the Depression—even the political results—now demand interpretation in light of the impact on family values and roles. Or, somewhat more grandiosely, the meaning of the Enlightenment now requires attention to childrearing practices, not only in the spread of new values through education and parental advice, but in the cause of new ideas through the complex reordering—and improvement—of the view of the basic nature of the human child in ordinary family behavior. In these cases and others, conventional history of the sort that sees politics causing politics, in a self-contained environment that rarely encompasses ordinary people or the non-political aspects of ordinary lives, is just not accurate any longer. The approach is also needlessly dull and lifeless, and it should not be endured since it is also incorrect. This is one aspect of the surge of social history at the research level that the schools cannot legitimately ignore. It is the clearest reason why even a back-to-basics movement must recognize that the history that must be presented—and memorized and digested—has changed during the past two decades.

To this, an interdisciplinary appeal can be added. Social history materials can allow some hope of a realistic combination of social science concerns and concepts with historical materials and methods. Criminology, demography, the sociology of medicine, and gerontology all now have clear branchings in solid sociohistorical work; so, of course, do stratification and mobility analysis and family sociology. Even psychology must increasingly come to terms with changes in fairly basic human relationships, including emotional intensity within the family, sexual habits, and personal privacy. It is not fanciful to project a school-level social history course serving as a vehicle for solid work in various social sciences connected by the effort to move across the various facets of a given society in a given period, and enriched by the juxtaposition of data from present and coherent past.

All of this remains, however, something of an undersell. The goals thus far suggested would benefit students exposed to school materials in social history, but as arguments would, I suspect, appeal to few of them. To be sure, the college historian who hopes to reach into the high schools is quickly told that it is not students he must persuade, but teachers. Still, an effort to rouse students to a new set of interests and involvements will surely be persuasive to their mentors as well; and, certainly, the heart of the effort to introduce students to the newest generation of sociohistorical concerns—the grasp of the historical dimension of the various facets of ordinary life and mentalities—lies in the building of a new kind of involvement in history.

For what social historians are now attempting is, in essence, the historical projection of the kinds of concerns most people have in shaping their own lives and in judging their own society. We clearly evaluate life today in terms of crime as well as political institutions; and we evaluate sports and health as well as the state of philosophy. But as a society we tend to bifurcate our evaluations, using at least some historical sense in the political and intellectual categories, but only a vague frame of reference for the rest.

One result, of course, is a set of errors in judgment; and not the least of the purposes of the introduction of social history in the schools is to challenge—and I would hope gradually to dislodge—these errors. Crime and the cities are not linked in any simple way; city growth, with all its tensions, has historically been compatible in a number of cases with a decline in crime. This is worth knowing, because it affects our evaluation of the inevitability of crime today. The family has not neatly moved from extended to nuclear, and relatedly the position of the elderly has not moved simply from veneration to rejection with the progress of modernization. These judgments, too, against a good bit of durable popular and journalistic (and, regrettably, still sociological) belief are important to convey at the high school level.

But even some vital rectifications do not constitute the main point. One moves closer in suggesting that the discussion of some of the more surprising sociohistorical findings—along with the increasing realization that aspects of human behavior we tend to regard as innate and therefore historyless, such as youthful romantic love as a felt emotion, are in fact products of past cultural constructs—is not only factually sound, but intriguing; and the discussion of the implications of the findings for the nature of contemporary life truly revealing. For the purpose of teaching social history—and, I believe, the real motivation for social history research and the cause of its growing crescendo—is the confrontation of what our society is like with how it got that way. It requires an assessment of our own values, in aspects of life that should be discussed rather than assumed.

LEVELS OF SOCIAL HISTORY

This claim can be briefly analyzed at three related levels. First, many of the subjects of social history, given the steady widening of topical range, fall into categories that we normally subject to an implicit historical judgment. Newspaper fare regularly suggests problems in crime levels or family life on the basis of assumptions about the past. Politicians now routinely comment on phenomena such as a decline in the work ethic, which is essentially a historical judgment. Less examined, but present, are assumptions about medical care or the growth of leisure activities. It is virtually impossible to gain much understanding in these human activities simply by examining and categorizing present patterns. There must be some sense of trend, some sense of how behavior is moving from past through present to, possibly, future. Except perhaps by comparative analysis, we have no idea whether our crime problems are good, bad, or indifferent unless we know what past levels involved. Historical thinking is thus almost inescapable when we try to assess the quality of our society. Yet, obviously, this thinking is rarely based on very serious research and operates often on an almost mythic plane. What social history teaching can do is simultaneously make explicit the need for historical thinking in these basic aspects of life and give some data, in key topical areas, for its enlightened conduct. Social historians judge past life, in other words, in much the same terms that we as laymen judge present life, and the linkage is vital to the lay judgment.

Social history also forces us to examine fundamental assumptions about the present in relationship to the past. If our beliefs about modern crime lead to sometimes excessive nostalgia about the past, some stickier instances derive from the more pervasive modern belief in progress. Two illustrations here, around the larger theme that the discussion of social-historical trends, and their openness to evaluation in terms of gain and loss, constitute a vital way for students to deal with their approach to key phenomena in modern life. The students need not change their approach, but they should be able to see their action as a social choice, not an immutable necessity.

Health levels undeniably constitute a modern success story in important respects. One has to cater to the belief in progress in recounting changes in mortality rates, even when this is qualified by noting the rather limited periods and somewhat limited age ranges in and for which the most dramatic gains were made. Readily enough might the rise of doctors and the displacing of superstition seem to parallel the history of health, a parallelism emphasized, in fact, in most conventional medical histories. The complete history, however, involves also the assessment of the rise of doctors and rise of the belief in doctors as social artifacts, not simply the empirical result of health or medical progress. Hence, for example, the attention to the professionalization process of the nineteenth century, or the faith-like quality of elements of belief in doctors in more recent decades. The purpose of analysis of this sort is first, of course, to provide a rounded historical assessment; and it is not designed to conduce toward any particular approach to doctors in contemporary society. But it *is* designed to conduce to thinking about one's own belief system and to understand it as a social product even when there is no desire or need to change it.

Serious researchers in the history of childhood have proclaimed the twentieth century as the first century in which children have been decently regarded and treated; so it is obvious that here, too, historical findings readily reinforce dominant beliefs about the brutalities of the past compared to modern enlightenment. As recent children, students might be expected to have their own empirical questions about the quality of modern childrearing; but, in fact, in class settings, they tend to mirror larger public beliefs about progress. Only with difficulty can they put modern problems in a more complicated context. Certainly, when the historian must introduce concepts like breaking the will, and practices like swaddling or wet-nursing, as characteristic of older forms of childrearing, the ability to complicate facile belief systems must be hard won. A major theme of the history of modern childhood in the Western world has to be the breaking down of a number of harsh disciplinary practices, including practices that contributed to massive child death rates; a related theme, less firm but certainly important for speculation, is the rise of deeper, more pervasive love for children. All of this seems so clearly good, so clearly desirable, that it might seem difficult to use this particular historical theme to obtain anything but the most benign and self-congratulatory perspective on ourselves in our relationship to the past.

This is, of course, precisely where more complex perspective is particularly needed. Teachers of social history must convey a number of undoubted improvements in childrearing as facts. As with medicine, their purpose need not at all promote a reversal of modern beliefs; but their purpose most definitely is to promote serious thinking about these beliefs. In the present case, this can begin with the juxtaposition of some glaring modern problems in childhood with the apparent historical record of progress. If childrearing has improved so much, why the massive rise, in modern society, of adolescent suicide? Why the broader tendency to view adolescents as troublesome and, indeed, the modern need to invent the whole concept of adolescence as a particularly troubled period of life? From this, it becomes valid to discuss some of the advantages of older, apparently harsher, childrearing methods: the absence of pronounced identity crises, for example, in a society where children associated less completely with peers and more regularly with adults whose lives they were expected to imitate. It becomes valid to consider the drawbacks that attend some apparent modern advantages: more love for children sounds great, but how does it mesh with the exposure of older children to unprecedentedly impersonal institutions? It would doubtless be appalling to produce a class of budding social history addicts bent on restoring past standards of childhood, but this development is unlikely. Nevertheless, a chance to view modern conventions of childhood with a bit of detachment, to see them as sources of some quite familiar problems as well as benefits, can only be enlightening. Such enlightenment might, to some extent, make the drawbacks a bit easier to modify in our own social future.

The purpose, again, is a simple one. Some basic impulses in modern society are so deeply rooted that we grow up viewing them as virtually inevitable: for example, more medicine for better health, or more love for better childhoods. Social history, devoted to these topics, shows the trends as social artifacts. It does not thereby prove them undesirable; but it does subject them to a new kind of understanding, and that kind of understanding—which really involves how our present stems from our past—is surely a basic goal of history education.

Sometimes this purpose can be extended more personally and beyond a general historical framework for evaluating basic features of our social life. The social history of leisure, which has opened up so excitingly in recent years, gives clear substance to the frequent claim that modern people are uncertain, individually as well as collectively, about what purpose leisure is supposed to serve. For we are legitimately unsure whether leisure is supposed to be fun, a dramatic contrast to work, or devoted to self-improvement and enhancement of an ability to work. Leisure is not, of course, very explicitly discussed in the schools in any fashion, so it is already a gain simply to bring it to the attention of students as a topic that deserves analysis. By dealing with it historically, a student has an opportunity to hone his or her own sense of what leisure purposes should be, not in terms of absolute rights and wrongs—which students produce readily, but often meaninglessly—but in terms of the real social constraints and opportunities of modern life. Social history does not tell students how to choose proper leisure values or family values or work values. But good social history teaching does force students to consider what values they want for themselves, and, to an extent, what difficulties they might encounter in modern society in pursuing them.

On several levels, then, social history promotes intelligent discussion of values. The result can engage at least some students in a new realization of the relevance of historical understanding. It can catch some up short by opening to serious inquiry topics that are never discussed with any sense of context at any stage of the educational process. The demands which this process can place on the teacher, in knowledge but also in a high level of sensitivity, are great. The result can be little short of glorious: the promotion of new insight into the forces that shape fundamental features of modern human life. If this seems too grandiose a claim, it can be put more prosaically. Any historian who has discussed some of the new themes of social history with an adult audience has inevitably encountered the reaction—really the lament: "I didn't know that was history." I take the lament to mean something more than a factual statement that current historical research topics were not part of history course fare in the past. I think it means that adults can perceive that this newer history really does illumine key aspects of the human experience. It provides, at least for some, a means of personal understanding. It is this understanding, along with an important new range of facts and concepts, that must, I believe, be made available as part of the school-derived definition of what history is.

CONCLUSION

This chapter has not directly claimed that social history will attract more student devotion than ordinary history does. This may be a logical conclusion from my assessment of the relevance of social history to an understanding of the world we operate in; but the problem is empirical, and on this we must await more data from actual tests of new curricular materials. Judging by college teaching experience, some students will be drawn to the stuff of social history who are repelled by the elitist, or formalistic, or lifeless qualities of some conventional history. Others will be a bit confused by the absence of clear dates and processions of names. Social history is in some ways harder than regular history, calling on a higher learning level, or at least on an ability to identify different kinds of facts; and this challenge, along with unfamiliarity, might deter some. Some students can't be interested in any kind of history, and some probably can't be interested in much of anything. There is no need to be Panglossian in our assessment of social history's wonder-working in the schools.

Even if they do not include claims of assured popularity, the justifications for reorienting history teaching toward more social history are compelling. Social history really does aid human understanding. It really does force consideration of issues and values vital to thinking about what life consists of, now as well as in the past. The statement of the values implication of social history is really a statement that the excitement of the best social history research—the sense of discovery of what makes real people tick—can and must be conveyed in teaching. We have the basis now for a much fuller sense of how the present relates to the past, of where we have come from to get where we are. It is imperative that the kind of thinking involved in this broadening of history—the sense that the present can be judged, in virtually all its aspects, by an understanding of its historical provenance—along with some of the principal factual discoveries of social history, be conveyed in the schools. Social history research has long had a missionary quality, a sense of opening vast new windows onto the past. It is time to impart this same quality to history teaching.

BIBLIOGRAPHY

For fuller discussions of the nature of social history, see Harold Perkin, "Social History," in H. Finberg, ed., *Approaches to History* (Toronto: University of Toronto Press, 1962); and Peter N. Stearns, "Toward a Wider Vision: Trends in Social History," in Michael Kammen, ed., *The Past Before Us* (Ithaca: Cornell University Press, 1980).

Many leading developments in social history can be followed through key journals in the field: *Journal of Social History, Comparative Studies in Society and History, Journal of Interdisciplinary History,* and *Past and Present.*

College-level surveys in social history include John R. Gillis, *The Development of European Society, 1770-1870* (Boston: Houghton Mifflin, 1977); Peter N. Stearns, *European Society in Upheaval; Social History since 1750* (New York: Macmillan, 1975); and Eric Hobshawn, *Age of Revolution, 1789-1848* (New York: Mentor, 1969). The United States is less well served, but see Robert Wiebe, *The Segmented Society* (New York: Oxford University Press, 1975) and Richard Brown, *Modernization: The Transformation of American Life* (New York: Hill and Wang, 1976).

Useful readers in the field are Gary B. Nash and Thomas R. Frazier, *The Private Side of American History* (2 volumes, New York: Harcourt Brace Jovanovich, 1979) and Stanley Chodorow and Peter N. Stearns, *The Other Side of Western Civilization* (2 volumes, New York: Harcourt Brace Jovanovich, 1979).

A variety of monographs, important in themselves, give much of the flavor of social history. On the United States, Philip Greven, *The Protestant Temperament* (New York: Alfred A. Knopf, 1978) and Carl Degler, *At Odds: Women and Family Life* (New York: Oxford University Press, 1980) are recent contributions in family history See also William Chafe, *Women and Equality, Changing Patterns in American Culture* (New York: Oxford University Press, 1977) and Peter N. Stearns, *Be a Man: Males in Modern Society* (New York: Holmes & Meier, 1979). On age groupings, Joseph Kett, *Rites of Passage: Adolescence in America, 1790 to the Present* (New York: Basic Books, 1977) and W. Andrew Achenbaum, *Old Age in the New Land* (Baltimore: Johns Hopkins University Press, 1979). Social mobility has been much studied: Stephan Thernstrom, *Poverty and Progress, Social Mobility in a Nineteenth Century City* (Cambridge: Harvard University Press, 1964) and *The Other Bostonians: Poverty and Progress in the American Metropolis* (Cambridge: Harvard University Press, 1973); Peter R. Decker, *Fortunes and Failures; White-Collar Mobility in 19th Century San Francisco* (Cambridge: Harvard University Press, 1978); and John Bodnar, Roger Simon, and Michael Weber, *Lives of Their Own* (Urbana: University of Illinois

Press, 1982). On other key social history topics: Eugene D. Genovese, *Roll, Jordan, Roll: The World the Slaves Made* (New York: Pantheon Books, 1974); Michael Katz, *Class, Bureaucracy and the Schools; The Illusion of Educational Change in America* (New York: Praeger, 1975); Richard W. Fox, *So Far Disordered in Mind; Insanity in California, 1870-1930* (Berkeley, University of California Press, 1979); Susan Reversby and David R. Romer, *Health Care in America: Essays in Social History* (Philadelphia: Temple University Press, 1978); Roger Lane, *Violent Death: The Social Significance of Suicide, Accident and Murder in 19th Century Philadelphia* (Cambridge: Harvard University Press, 1980); David Johnson, *Crime and Law Enforcement: A History* (St. Louis: Forum Press, 1981); Paul E. Johnson, *A Shopkeeper's Millennium: Society and Revivals in Rochester, N.Y., 1815-1837* (New York: Hill and Wang, 1978); and David Stannard, *The Puritan Way of Death: A Study in Religion, Culture and Social Change* (New York: Oxford University Press, 1977).

Special topics in European social history reveal slightly different patterns, emphasizing class structure, protest, and leisure, for example, more than American work does. There are topical overlaps as well, of course. On preindustrial society, Peter Laslett, *The World We Have Lost* (New York: Scribner, 1965) and Natalie Z. Davis, *Society and Culture in Early Modern France* (Stanford: Stanford University Press, 1975). On protest, Charles Tilly, Louise Tilly, and Richard Tilly, *The Rebellious Century, 1803-1930* (Cambridge: Harvard University Press, 1975) is a good introduction. Michael Marrus, *The Rise of Leisure in Industrial Society* (St. Louis: Forum Press, 1974); Robert Malcolmson, *Popular Recreations in English Society, 1700-1850* (Cambridge, England: Cambridge University Press, 1973); Peter Bailey, *Leisure and Class in Victorian England* (Toronto: University of Toronto Press, 1978); and James Walton, *The Blackpool Landlady* (Liverpool: Liverpool University Press, 1979). On social class, the most influential single work has been E. P. Thompson, *The Making of the English Working Class* (New York: Pantheon Books, 1963); see also John Merriman, *Consciousness and Class Experience in 19th Century Europe* (New York: Holmes & Meier, 1980) and Theodore Zelden, *France, 1848-1945* (2 volumes, New York: Oxford University Press, 1979-1980).

On other special topics: A. N. Galpern, *The Religions of the People in 16th Century Champagne* (Cambridge: Harvard University Press, 1976); Emmanuel LeRoy Ladurie, *The Peasants of Languedoc* (Urbana: University of Illinois Press, 1973); Eugen Weber, *Peasants into Frenchman: The Modernization of Rural France* (Stanford: Stanford University Press, 1976); George Rosen, *Madness in Society: Chapters in the Historical Sociology of Mental Illness* (Chicago: University of Chicago Press, 1968); Philippe Ariès, *Centuries of Childhood: A Social History of Family Life* (New York: Random House, 1962) and *Western Attitudes toward Death* (Baltimore: Johns Hopkins University Press, 1974); J. H. Plumb, *The New World of Children*

(Cambridge, England: Cambridge University Press, 1976); Lawrence Stone, *The Family, Sex, and Marriage in England, 1500–1800* (New York: Harper & Row, 1977); Howard Zehr, *Crime and the Development of Modern Society* (Totowa, N.J.: Rowman and Littlefield, 1976); John Jacob Tobias, *Crime and Industrial Society in the 19th Century* (New York: Schocken Books, 1967); Patricia Branca, *Silent Sisterhood: Middle-Class Women in the Victorian Home* (Pittsburgh: Carnegie-Mellon University Press, 1975); Louise Tilly and Joan W. Scott, *Women, Work and Family* (New York: Holt, Rinehart and Winston, 1978); Peter N. Stearns, *Old Age in European Society* (New York: Holmes & Meier, 1977); John R. Gillis, *Youth and History: Tradition and Change in European Age Relations* (New York: Academic Press, 1973).

Finally, a deservedly popular book that captures many of the themes of social history in a local context: Emmanuel LeRoy Ladurie, *Montaillou: The Promised Land of Error* (New York: Braziller, 1979). First-rate American local studies that contribute to a definition of social history's topics and methods include Philip Greven, *Four Generations: Population, Land and Family in Colonial Andover, Massachusetts* (Ithaca: Cornell University Press, 1970); John Demos, *A Little Commonwealth: Family Life in Plymouth Colony* (New York: Oxford University Press, 1970); Tamara Hareven and Philip Langenbach, *Amoskeag* (New York: Pantheon Books, 1979); and Anthony F. C. Wallace, *Rockdale: The Growth of an American Village in the Early Industrial Revolution* (New York: Alfred A. Knopf, 1978).

SUGGESTIONS FOR TEACHING SOCIAL HISTORY

Translating Social History for the Classroom

LINDA W. ROSENZWEIG

The "basics" of the human past—those elements of past experience that represent the fundamentals of ordinary life, and their impact on society—ought to have a place in the curricula of our high schools. American history is an integral component of most secondary curricula, and it is imperative as well as appropriate that the key approaches and findings of social history become part of that component. The challenge is, of course, how to translate effectively the growing body of data about the "basics" of human experience into suitable and interesting curricular materials for high school students. With the exception of scattered references in some textbooks, this translation has not yet occurred.

How can social history be taught at the high school level? Can sophisticated generalizations, even about familiar phenomena and activities—such as family life and work—be made meaningful to the majority of students who think of history as names, dates, and events to be memorized, or, perhaps, to be charted on a time line? Can social history be made interesting to students who have never been asked to examine the experiences of groups or to consider the implications of past social trends for contemporary life? Will these students be comfortable with "facts" of social history which are different from the facts they are used to learning?

One way to begin to make students comfortable with a new approach to historical study is to build on areas which are already established in the secondary curriculum. Family history, for example, has become an increasingly popular topic at the high school level. The study of family history can easily be extended from a focus on personal history—or the "Roots" approach—to a broader examination of the social history of family life in America. As a follow-up to compiling personal family histories, students might be introduced to several of the concepts used by social historians in their investigations of family life in the past and be invited to apply them to the data they have collected. Thus, the notions of family function, family roles, and affectional relations might be developed through a series of questions. What does a family do? What specific things does each family member do? What holds the family together? Students can apply these questions first to their own contemporary families, then to the data that they have gathered concerning previous generations of their own families, and eventually to material concerning other families in their historical contexts. They might, for example, examine Benjamin Franklin's family as depicted in his autobiography.

There are several sources of background information on the social history of the family. Among the most useful are: Carl Degler, *At Odds: Women and the Family in America from the Revolution to the Present* (New York: Oxford University Press, 1980); Michael Gordon, ed., *The American Family in Socio-Historical Perspective*, 2nd ed. (New York: St. Martin's Press, 1977). Other titles can be found in the annotated bibliography to Chapter 2 of this Bulletin.

The Industrial Revolution offers another example of a topic covered in most American history courses that can serve as an effective springboard for the integration of social history into the curriculum. Students' understanding of the impact of industrialization, the rise of the factory system, and the mechanization of production can be enhanced significantly by contrasting these developments with characteristic preindustrial patterns of work and leisure. Students would find striking differences in the family as a production unit, the predominance of manual labor, the mingling of work and leisure, the relative stability of the work pattern for most people, and the degree of control which individuals exercised over their work lives. Useful sources for the teacher on the social history of work and leisure and the contrast between preindustrial work and work in industrial society include: Peter Laslett, *The World We Have Lost* (New York: Scribner's, 1965); Daniel Rodgers, *The Work Ethic in Industrial America* (Chicago: University of Chicago Press, 1971); Herbert G. Gutman, *Work, Culture and Society in Industrializing America* (New York: Random House, 1976); and Thomas Dublin, *Women at Work* (New York: Columbia University Press, 1979). A unit that draws upon such books to compare aspects of social history in industrial and preindustrial America will place the Industrial Revolution in much sharper perspective.

A major effort to translate current sociohistorical scholarship for classroom use is in progress in the form of a three-year curriculum development and in-service training project based at Carnegie-Mellon University. The Project on Social History, supported by the National Endowment for the Humanities, has produced an introductory unit on the nature of social history and five curriculum units on major social history themes: family, childhood, work and leisure, health and medicine, and crime and law enforcement. Each of the five thematic units consists of twenty lessons which trace the history of the unit topic from the preindustrial period to contemporary society.

The units are self-contained, and they can be used in various ways, in part or as a whole. Examples are drawn from both American and European contexts in an effort to make the materials useful in history courses in both areas, as well as in other social studies courses. Thus, a teacher of American history might use all of the material in a given unit as the basis for a minicourse, emphasizing the American manifestations of a particular phenomenon—such as the evolution of modern health conditions and the growth of the medical profession—and select some European examples for comparison and contrast. Similarly, all five units could be integrated to build a full course in American history or modern social history.

A more selective utilization of the materials is also possible. A teacher might choose specific lessons from one or more of the units, possibly those on health conditions in the New World, childrearing in the colonies, or family life as illustrated through a case study of Benjamin Franklin's family, to supplement the study of the colonial period in an American history survey course. In the same way, individual lessons from one or more of the units could be integrated with other pertinent material. For example, lessons on the decline of leisure and changing crime patterns could be used in conjunction with the study of the Industrial Revolution.

The Project on Social History's curriculum units address the question of how can social history be done through a set of nine teaching approaches: chronological organization; narrative readings; pictures, graphs, and other documentary sources; individual and small-group work; inquiry; written assignments; lectures; comparison of students' own personal experiences with the experiences of people in the past; and examination of value-related issues in historical contexts. While these approaches are not new to the classroom or unique to the teaching of social history, they do reflect the staff's attempt to present information in a variety of appropriate formats and to identify teaching strategies which will help students to cope with historical study that emphasizes group experiences, trends, and processes rather than individuals and events.

The lessons that follow illustrate typical activities representative of the Project's approach to the teaching of social history. While both lessons are integral parts of the respective units in which they appear, each can be utilized as a self-contained lesson in the context of an American history course.

The first lesson is taken from the Project's unit "The History of Childhood in Western Europe and the United States, 1630–1980." It asks students to compare preindustrial American and European childrearing practices by reading a series of letters and recording their conclusions on a chart. For background information, the teacher may wish to refer to the following sources of additional information on the history of childhood: Philippe Ariès, *Centuries of Childhood: A Social History of Family Life* (New York: Random House, 1962); Robert H. Bremner et al., eds., *Children and Youth in America: A Documentary History* (Cambridge: Harvard University Press, Massachusetts, 1970); and Philip Greven, *The Protestant Temperament: Patterns of Child-Rearing, Religious Experience and the Self in Early America* (New York: Alfred A. Knopf, 1978).

Lesson One: Childrearing in America and Europe in the Preindustrial Period

INTRODUCTION

Although European and American children experienced generally similar childhoods in the preindustrial period, there were some significant differences. Europeans travelling in America could easily detect these differences. For example, Americans did not swaddle their children. This is a simple enough distinction on the surface, but what does it suggest about parents' attitudes, and the personalities of children? There were other specific differences separating American from European childrearing practices. A closer look at colonial life reveals a life style allowing different childrearing attitudes and practices in the New World.

As you read the following letters, written to her sister Susannah by a European woman who was visiting another sister in America, see if you can identify some of these practices and some possible reasons for them.*

LETTER 1

Salem, Massachusetts
April 1687

Dear Susannah,

What a relief, after the long boat trip, to arrive safely in America! Sarah and her family were excited to see me, not only because we have been separated for so long, but also because they have so little company. Their farm has acres and acres of land, with more available cheaply, and for that we can envy them. But Sarah is so far away from her neighbors! The closest neighbor is a half hour buggy ride away. It seems that most families here left their kin in Europe, so I suppose that makes Sarah cherish her family all the more.

In spite of the distance between farms, everyone in Salem looks out for his neighbor. I hear stories about people from all different classes helping each other when they build a house or care for the sick. I am also amazed that even indentured servants can become comfortable farmers by working hard. Who knows what opportunities Sarah's new little baby might have, if he lives?

I am grateful that I could come to help Sarah when the baby comes. I am surprised that she is not more fearful of the event, but even looks forward to it. (But then, Sarah always was the independent one of us, wasn't she? I suppose that is what gave her the courage to move to the New World. She seems willing to accept the new ideas necessary to adjusting to life here.) She also trusts the midwife, assuring me that the American midwives are better trained than ours. Still, I am relieved to be here, in case she needs help. The little graveyard reminds us that not all babies live. But sometimes even the

---

*Although these letters are similar to letters written during the colonial period, they were written by Lenore Schneider, author of the Project's unit on childhood.

men here weep at the death of a child, as if they had more hope for its survival than we can expect in Europe.

Affectionately yours,

Abigail

LETTER 2

Salem, Massachusetts
May 1687

Dear Susannah,

Sarah bore a new son last week and so far they are both healthy. She and Matthew have already named the baby (Thomas), another sign that they expect him to live. I came prepared to take the tedious task of swaddling the baby each day, but Sarah said no, that she would let the baby be. Sarah plans to make time to watch her child. In other families older sisters take their turn—one good result of the larger families people have over here. I was watching Sarah with the baby today, and I marveled that she actually seems to delight in the wild wiggles his arms and legs make. Matthew is eager for the time when little Thomas can help with the milking.

My next surprise was that Sarah is nursing the child herself, rather than sending him out to wet nurse (of course they are not readily available in these isolated spots!). At first I pitied Sarah for not having servants, especially since she does not have the benefit of swaddling or a wet nurse. I have noticed, though, that she does not mind the extra time spent with the baby, and Matthew helps by playing with the older children, and giving them easy chores to do on the farm. Do you remember when I had to send my little Samuel to the countryside to strengthen his weak frame? Not so, here. In fact the Americans do not send their children out to other farms at all, but rather keep them to work on the family farm.

Affectionately yours,

Abigail

LETTER 3

Salem, Massachusetts
July 1687

Dear Susannah,

Judging from your response to my letter, you fear that Sarah and Matthew have abandoned our traditions in bringing up their children. It is true that the baby does not have to submit to swaddling, and the older children are not whipped every time they are obstinate or misbehave. Why, just today, little Edward spoke sharply to his sister Anne and shoved her against the chair. Rather then using the rod against Edward (as so many Europeans would do), Matthew shamed him into confession and repentance, in such a firm way that I do not think Edward likely to repeat the offense.

But lest you think that they have drifted from the Puritan faith and practice, you should know that Sarah and Matthew continue in the church, and, with the other members, hope that Salem will set an example for other communities. What a difference from most Europeans! Each family here still has its own worship time at home every day, with Bible reading. Even school helps to set the children in the right ways, for they are taught not to cheat, lie, steal or to dance. New England children are "swaddled in Calvinism," I think, for their religion helps to control the children until such time as self-control can rule their actions. How much harder it is for our own children to continue on the right path, considering the worldly influences so readily available in Europe.

Affectionately yours,

Abigail

LETTER 4

Salem, Massachusetts
August 1687

Dear Susannah,
As proud as I am of sister Sarah and her children's upbringing, I was disquieted to learn that not all parents have Puritan ideas about childrearing. Parents in the Southern colonies, for example, expect their slaves to help discipline the children, and the slaves are not nearly as strict as we would be. Even if the tendency for indulgence is only in the genteel class, I fear that it will spread to others. I am sending you an article, printed in the Virginia Gazette, and I am sure that you will be as shocked as I was at such laxity in discipline. (From the Virginia Gazette)

"One distinguished gentleman visited friends in the countryside, expecting to spend a relaxing weekend. He describes his experience as quite the opposite, however: On my arrival here I found a house full of children, who are humoured beyond measure, and indeed absolutely spoiled by the ridiculous indulgence of a fond mother. . . . The second day of my visit, in the midst of dinner, the eldest boy, who is eight years old, whipped off my periwig with great dexterity, and received the applause of the table for his humor and spirit . . . . Six of the children are permitted to sit at the table, who entirely monopolize the wings of fowls and the most delicate morsels of every dish because the mother has discovered that her children have not strong stomachs. In the morning, before my friend is up, I generally take a turn upon the gravel walk, where I could wish to enjoy my own thoughts without interruption; but I am here instantly attended by my little tormentors, who follow me backwards and forwards, and play at what they call Running after the Gentleman. My whip, which was a present from an old friend, has been lashed to pieces by one of the boys, who is fond of horses; and the handle is *turned into a hobby horse . . . . The mother's attention to the children entirely destroys all conversation; and once as an amusement for the evenings, we attempted to begin reading, but were interrupted, in the second page, by little Sammy, who is suffered to whip his top in the parlour . . . and a little miss, at breakfast, is allowed to drink up all the cream, and put her fingers into the sugar dish, because she was once sickly . . . . It is whispered in the family that I am a mighty good sort of a man, but that I cannot talk to children."*

Can you imagine such behavior being allowed in our town? Certainly not! We must be sure to break the will of our children, not allow them to rule us!

Affectionately yours,

Abigail

SUMMARY QUESTIONS

1. What basis did seventeenth-century Europeans have for saying that Americans were strongly child-centered?
2. If you were a new European immigrant to America in the seventeenth century and wanted to choose the best child-rearing methods from each culture, which ones would you select, and why?
3. Write a letter to a European relative explaining what it is like to be a youth in preindustrial society.

The second lesson, an activity taken from the Project on Social History's unit *Work and Leisure in History*, is based on an excerpt from Studs Terkel's *Working* (New York: Pantheon, 1974). The complete lesson includes a narrative section which outlines the growth of retirement since 1900 and highlights some of the issues raised as retirement has become increasingly common. Teachers may wish to refer to W. Andrew Achenbaum, *Old Age in the New Land* (Baltimore: Johns Hopkins University Press, 1979) and Gail Buchwalter King and Peter N. Stearns, "The Retirement Experience as a Policy Factor: An Applied History Approach," *Journal of Social History*, Summer, 1981, pp. 589–625, to prepare a background lecture before introducing the activity.

Lesson Two: A Case Study of Retirement

Students should read Studs Terkel's interview with Joe Zmuda, pp. 562–567, in which Mr. Zmuda discusses his experiences during the ten years since his voluntary retirement.

SOCIAL HISTORY AND THE TEACHING OF HISTORY

Use the excerpt from *Working* as a case study to illustrate the experience of one retired worker. After students have completed the reading, focus discussion on issues such as:
- Why did Mr. Zmuda retire?
- How did he feel about his decision at the time?
- How did he feel when Studs Terkel interviewed him?
- How did Mr. Zmuda spend most of his time after retirement?
- What sorts of things did he look forward to?
- What can you infer about retirement in general from his comments?
- How typical do you think his experiences were?

Based on what you have read about Mr. Zmuda, do you think retirement is a good thing for most workers? Why or why not? What are some of the limitations of a case study with regard to drawing general conclusions?

Ask students to interview a retired worker and compare his/her experiences and impressions with those of Mr. Zmuda. Prepare for the interviews by asking students to generate a list of questions they would like to ask. For example:
- What was your job?
- How long did you work?
- How long have you been retired?
- Did you retire voluntarily?
- How do you spend your time now?
- Are you satisfied with retirement? Why or why not?

Students might tape their interviews and play excerpts for the class or report orally on their findings. The class should compare the impressions they form from their own research with the material in the excerpt from *Working* and the information presented in the teacher's introductory lecture. If this case study has been preceded by discussions of work and leisure in earlier societies, particularly during the period of the Industrial Revolution, students should speculate about what current retirement patterns mean in terms of the evolution of work and leisure. Is retirement becoming more endurable and popular, and if so, is this because work is becoming less interesting, or because leisure is becoming more legitimate?

Conclude the activity with a discussion of the advantages and disadvantages of retirement in contemporary society.
- Is compulsory retirement a good thing? Why or why not?
- Does society have a right to force workers to retire?
- How might retirement programs be designed to respond more adequately to human needs?
- Would you want to retire? Why or why not?

For further information about the curriculum units developed by the Project on Social History, the reader may write to the Project on Social History, History Department, Carnegie-Mellon University, Schenley Park, Pittsburgh, PA 15213.

CHAPTER 4

Industrial America's Rank and File: Recent Trends in American Labor History

LEON FINK

AMERICAN LABOR HISTORY has undergone "striking" changes in the past fifteen years. Not only the questions asked, but the subject matter under study have shifted dramatically over a very short period. From a focus on unions and their leaders, what had once been a fairly tightly-constructed subsection of economic and political history has branched out in a number of new directions. In particular, labor historians have recently had a great deal to say about three vital areas of the American experience: the changing nature of work and the workplace, the forms and logic of working-class organization, and the impact of labor history, or "the worker's presence," on American history generally. Formative influences on these developments have included the renewal of popular movements (often outside established centers of power and organization) in the 1960s; the publication of E.P. Thompson's *The Making of the English Working Class* (1963), exemplary both for the passion and sensitivity of its Marxist approach; as well as the general assimilation into the historical discipline of social science methodologies in the form of quantification and sociological-anthropological theories and model-building. To a significant extent, labor history has thus become one of the mainsprings within the larger field of social history; indeed, some practitioners now prefer to identify themselves as "working-class social historians."[1]

The combination of quantitative sources (especially the manuscript census, city directories, and tax records) with an imaginative use of other archival records has with great effectiveness brought to life the world of the

---

[1] For other useful overviews of developments within labor history, see David Montgomery, "To Study the People: The American Working Class," *Labor History* 21 (Fall 1980): 485–512; David Brody, "The Old Labor History and the New," *Labor History* 20 (1979): 111–26; and D. Fahey, "From Labor History to Working Class History," *Journal of Urban History* 6 (Nov. 1979): 105–11.

lower classes from eighteenth century artisans, slaves, and indentured servants to the craft and factory workers of the nineteenth century. For the twentieth century, the addition of oral testimony has likewise begun to yield rich rewards. The so-called "inarticulate" of history have all too often simply gone uncataloged, unstudied, or unremembered. For a good example of a new use of a standard source of labor history, we might look at what has recently been done with the formal records and proceedings of the Knights of Labor, the largest and most significant labor organization of the nineteenth century. Norman Ware (1929) and Gerald Grob (1961) put parts of this incredible collection of materials—now grouped on dozens of microfilm reels under the Terence Powderly Papers—to use in most effective institutional histories of the Knights. More recently, however, the official records of this labor body, together with the vast incoming correspondence to its leaders, have been combed for an understanding of the kinds of people who joined the organization, their concerns, their aspirations, and their problems in specific local contexts. Much of this work, circulating in the papers and dissertations of young scholars, remains to be published; but it has been helped immeasurably by Jonathan Garlock's and N.C. Builder's (1973) quantitative guide to every known local outpost of this social movement.[2]

WORK OF HERBERT GUTMAN

Of the several distinguished North American scholars who have charted the way towards a "new" labor history, Herbert Gutman (1976) has shown most dramatically the changing preoccupations of the field. Gutman's early work, at least in its point of departure, bears the strong imprint of the categories of economic history through which most studies of labor movements had been conceived. Still, from the start, Gutman had brought a new perspective to his material. Assessing the reaction of different groups of workers to the depression of the 1870s, Gutman quickly found that neither the swings of the business cycle nor the fluctuation of the labor market adequately accounted for the relative abilities of some workers to sustain a considerable measure of influence in their relations with employers. Rather, the larger relationship of a given body of workers to the surrounding community (i.e., other workers, shopkeepers, local officeholders, police, etc.) might prove equally decisive in industrial battles. This initial work propelled Gutman further into the complexities of the social structure and culture of industrial America. For example, he found that the competitive individualism and success ideology which had frequently been taken as the cultural masthead of the Gilded Age were at odds with other traditions and values which also carried considerable contemporary appeal. Taking his cue from

---

[2]See, e.g., Melton A. McLaurin, *The Knights of Labor in the South* (Westport, CT: Greenwood, 1978); Michael J. Cassity, "Modernization and Social Crisis: The Knights of Labor and a Midwestern Community, 1885–1886," *The Journal of American History*, 66 (June 1979): 41–61; and Leon Fink, "Irrespective of Party, Color or Social Standing: The Knights of Labor and Opposition Politics in Richmond, Virginia," *Labor History* 19 (Summer 1978): 325–49.

Thompson, Gutman pursued the idea that "behind every form of direct popular action, some legitimizing notion of right is to be found." From the symbols of a common culture, in fact, workers often drew quite different inspiration from their middle-class contemporaries. Evangelical Protestantism, Gutman discovered, sustained doctrines of trade unionism and mutualism, as well as laissez-faire economics and the Gospel of Wealth. One of those whose work fit the former category was Richard L. Davis, a black coal miners' leader and UMW officer from the Ohio Hocking Valley. Davis's own career, as Gutman elucidated it, also belied the historiographic image of a docile, anti-union Black labor force in the "age of Booker T. Washington."

As was the case with black coal miners, the specific social contours of the communities that Gutman studied continued to raise new questions. Beginning with his extensive work on Paterson, New Jersey, Gutman came to see the open conflict and considerable violence of the Gilded Age as a function of the attempt by a new class of industrial entrepreneurs to socialize and gain control over a diverse, discordant, but often resistant populace. Gutman found two important bases of opposition to the consolidating economic and political needs of the corporate capitalist order in the preindustrial and/or immigrant background of America's new factory recruits. From the farm women of Lowell to Afro-American slaves and Irish canal-diggers, from Welsh miners to Slavic steelworkers and Jewish seamstresses, the oft-mentioned "problem" of the American work ethic has masked a continuing cultural, as well as political-economic, battle between owners and policymakers, on the one hand, and workers, on the other. Having considered the cultural forms of working-class resistance, Gutman has most recently extended his investigation to include a group of workers debarred from overt workplace and political organization—namely, the Afro-American slaves. Here (1976), in a work which showed how far from their point of origin the concerns of a labor historian had led (and appropriately so), Gutman documented how the creation and defense—against all external obstacles—of coherent and distinct Afro-American family networks laid the basis for the survival and resistance of a people during and after slavery.

FOCUSING ON THREE MAJOR AREAS

It is worth looking in turn at the three major areas of recent focus—namely, work, worker organization and motivation, and the worker's impact on American life. The first area has yielded a particularly rich analysis of the changing shape of America's industrial revolution. In general, a picture of a continuous, but erratic and uneven, appropriation by management from workers of the knowledge and day-to-day direction of the production process has emerged from this literature. An exemplary study of this transformation of American working life is found in Alan Dawley's treatment of shoemaking in Lynn (1976).

In a story extending from the turn-of-the-century through the Gilded Age, Dawley presents a vivid picture of the steady erosion and ultimate decimation of an earlier artisan way of life. In 1800, the household served as the basic unit of shoe production. The master shoemaker (and head of the household) purchased the leather and supervised production in a "ten-footer" behind his family's cottage. Working under him were a couple of journeymen (usually younger) who brought their own kit of tools with them and who received from the master not only wages, but room and board, firewood, and clothing. Within the master's house, wives and daughters, working as binders, hand-stitched the upper part of the shoe. Younger sons, serving as apprentices and entrusted with a variety of odd jobs, completed the work team.

Household production was characterized by the unity of home and work life, as well as by control by the artisan of the work process and work day. Although each household contained an internal hierarchy, interdependence and a rough equality characterized the relations among shoeworking households and, indeed, between shoeworking households and most of the other households (farmers, craftsmen, small shopkeepers) of the "republican" community.

By the 1830s, household shoe production had given way to the central shop. The master, who had fashioned his finished goods on customer order or else sold them to a small shopkeeper, had fallen victim to his supplier and distributor. Taking advantage of credit and access to a protected national market, Lynn shopkeepers now took sole command of production. Their general stores became the center of a vast putting-out system, a characteristic part of the "middle passage" of United States industrialism. The central shop system expanded the scale and lowered the cost of shoe production. By loosening the ties between work and home, it helped to "free" the individual, narrowing the relation between employer and worker to the wage payment.

The real production explosion occurred in the 1860s, when the sewing machines and the McKay stitcher were combined with an intricate division of labor to create a factory system of mass production. Two thousand fewer workers produced seven million more shoes in 1875 than in 1855. The factory system had a drastic effect on the shoeworkers and their community. No natural line of mobility allowed the average worker to escape lifelong wage dependency. Fewer workers could expect to earn even a "competence"—"to possess real estate or saving sufficient to house a family, or tide it over during hard times, or support husband and wife in old age." A seasonal production cycle unleashed a vast army of tramps across the New England countryside. With the breakup of the shoeworking household, young men moved away from their parents, and the "lady shoebinder" gave way to the "factory girl," who left the labor market upon marriage.

Daily interaction between farmers and workers, men and women, children and adults, and dependent helpers and independent artisans in small-scale production had given way to a new order of work that stretched the ends of each of these polarities into separate social spheres. Workplace authority—previously exercised by the father or master craftsman or by one's fellow journeymen—for the first time yielded to external supervision in the person of the foreman.

Although we shall not here treat it in the same detail, a valuable body of scholarship also exists on the extension of the division of labor and managerialism into the workplaces of the twentieth century, as well. Richard Edwards (1979), for example, challenges the notion that the nature of industrial jobs and bureaucratic administration has moved along a smooth, technologically-defined continuum. Rather, Edwards argues that it has been the interaction of corporate practice with the responses of the workers themselves that has molded a dynamic managerial approach. In particular, he cites an evolution from simple (family firm) to hierarchical (foreman-run) control of industrial enterprise, increasingly complicated by resort to various union-evading strategems, such as welfare capitalism, scientific management, and company unions. Ultimately, monopoly sector firms resorted to a combination of "technical" (or machine-set pace of work) and "bureaucratic" (or complex organizational) forms of control over their work force.[3]

Among those who have most ably synthesized attention to the work process with the changing dimensions of the labor movement itself have been David Montgomery and David Brody. Along with Gutman, they have served over the last period as a kind of informal triumvirate giving coherence and direction to the discipline. Brody's seminal work on the steelworkers at the turn of the century (1960) analyzes the demise of the nation's strongest craft union in relation to the rising concentration of the steel industry, craft-union exclusiveness and native-immigrant conflict, and the effective use of the state's police power by the employers. In addition to wide-ranging investigations of social structure (1968) and social conflict (1972) within early nineteenth-century manufacturing centers, Montgomery (1979) has provided a most convincing portrait of the character of labor ideology, particularly among the skilled industrial craftsmen who lent leadership and stability to labor's organizational efforts, from the American Labor Union of the 1860s through the A.F. of L. and its anarcho-syndicalist critics early in the twentieth century. Amidst the changing technological and managerial constraints imposed from above, workers—first, as autonomous craftsmen; then through union work rules; and, finally, through sympathy strikes—struggled to maintain or regain control over decisions exercised on the shop floor. Montgomery argues that these control-oriented struggles, which crested in the unparalleled militancy of the years 1916–1920, had their roots in the craftsman's ethic of the work "stint" (the self-imposed limit on worker output), a defiant manliness in the face of unwarranted exactions from

---

[3]Other important works reflecting on changing authority within the twentieth-century workplace include: David F. Noble, *America By Design: Science, Technology, and the Rise of Corporate Capitalism* (New York: Basic Books, 1977); and Harry Braverman, *Labor and Monopoly Capital: The Degradation of Work in the Twentieth Century* (New York: Monthly Review Press, 1974). Contrast these to the happier picture presented by Daniel Nelson, *Managers and Workers: Origins of the New Factory System in the United States, 1880–1920* (Madison: University of Wisconsin Press, 1975).

above, and a disciplined solidarity with fellow workers.

That industrial resistance did not necessarily devolve from skill or "manly" assertion, however, has been skillfully documented by Thomas Dublin's recent work on the Lowell millworkers (1979). A work force recruited not from artisans, but from young, unmarried women of small New England farms nevertheless showed a capacity for collective action through the "turn-outs" of the 1830s and Ten Hour petitions of the 1840s. Rather than a tradition of craft, the Lowell women relied on a "sisterhood" formed in the common association of work, boarding house, and social life. A still-vibrant republican political tradition still had meaning for these Yankee daughters who would meet worsening industrial conditions with American Revolutionary invective:

We will show these drivelling cotton lords, this mushroom aristocracy of New England, who so arrogantly aspire to lord it over God's heritage, that our rights cannot be trampled upon with impunity; that we will not longer submit to that arbitrary power which has for last ten years been so abundantly exercised over us.[4]

In entirely different circumstances, a "workers' culture" among twentieth-century women department store workers, according to Susan Porter Benson (1978), continually frustrated managerial attempts at rationalization from above.

While it is true that, except for work on the early mill operatives, most scholarship has concentrated on those skilled trades that produced stable, or at least strong, unions, the analytic emphasis for the most part has been less on the unions themselves as historical agencies than on the larger environment which nourished them. Thus, as we have noted, there has been considerable attention devoted to the nature of the work process, with its changing skill requirements. The associational networks antedating as well as sustaining formal union organization have also figured prominently in the recent literature. Lodge meetings, voluntary fire companies, neighborhood taverns, as well as churches, ethnic societies, and political ward organizations, all played a role in the creation of cross-craft understanding and sympathy among urban workingmen. Many nineteenth-century studies, in particular, refer to the existence of a "working-class culture" which gave a meaning to contemporary values such as respectability, self-help, and even mobility, distinct from that applicable to its middle-class counterpart. Gregory Kealey's study (1980) of specific Toronto trades and social organization and Daniel Walkowitz's contrast of a mixed skilled-craft cotton town and a textile town in upstate New York (1978) offer particularly rich accounts of the larger associational world of organized workers in the late nineteenth-century.

The working-class community, as such, has been explored from a variety of angles. In his study of antebellum Lynn shoemakers, for example, Paul

---

[4]Caroline F. Ware, *The Early New England Cotton Manufacture* (Boston: Johnson Reprint Corp., 1931), p. 292.

Faler (1974) divided the shoeworking community into the three cultural categories of "traditionalists," "loyalists," and "rebels." Eschewing both the discipline of the new industrial morality and the radicals' efforts to organize for collective protection, the traditionalists stuck to the "looser," more casual, less routinized life style of the eighteenth-century workingman. The loyalists, on the other hand, bent to the standards of their new employers, embracing temperance and self-improvement, while likewise shunning labor organization. The rebel mechanics, while culturally indistinguishable from the loyalists, nevertheless turned a workplace morality conditioned by the labor theory of value, republicanism, and Christianity into a sharp critique of monopoly, exploitation, and political elitism.

Other authors have identified ethnicity as the basic reference point for workers' values. Contradicting older historiographic denigrations of the capacity for organization among lesser-skilled immigrant workers, Victor Greene portrays the militant coming-of-age of Slavic coal miners in Pennsylvania. In a wave of strikes near the end of the century, whole communities found inspiration both in the words of their priests and in the new political rights beckoning in the symbol of the American flag. Through an astute use of oral history, Peter Friedlander (1975), in a study of the organization of an auto-workers local in 1930s, and Nell Painter (1979), in her collaboration with the southern black Communist organizer Hosea Hudson, have also produced searching explorations of the intersection of the forces of ethnicity (or race) and class among American workers. Particularly in periods of weak labor organization, as David Montgomery (1972), among others, has demonstrated, ethnic rivalry and racial antagonisms among workers have come to the fore. But besides the complex question of whether ethnic consciousness reinforced or undermined "class consciousness" in America is the even more basic question of what impact ethnic identity had on working-class behavior. Virginia Yans-McLaughlin (1977), for example, has found that work and occupational decisions among Italians in Buffalo were conditioned by sex-role proprieties shaped in the Old Country. While Italian-American men gravitated towards outdoor work as construction laborers, women were culturally forbidden to leave home as domestics or factory workers, except under adequate familial (i.e., patriarchal) supervision, and only so long as female wages did not exceed those of male family members.

The study of unions themselves, a sustaining center of interest, at least for twentieth-century labor historians, has itself undergone a changing emphasis in recent years. Labor history in the United States in part was born out of the attempts of progressive-era labor economists to defend and justify the existence of organized labor within liberal capitalist society. By the 1960s, both the permanence of the unions and the failings of that society were taken for granted by many labor historians. As such, the unions themselves generally received critical scrutiny as established institutions. The growth of labor bureaucracy, "corporate ideology," opportunism, and corruption within major unions were emphasized, even as more radical rank-and-file efforts throughout the century were exhumed for future emulation.[5] Ironically, the declining economic strength and political influence of the labor movement amidst the stagflation of the 1970s has again touched off a scholarly revision of the unions' historic role. David Brody (1980) and James Green (1980) have offered the most mature, balanced syntheses extant on the twentieth-century experience of American unions. Meanwhile, excellent studies have also been written on such varied, specific topics as the career of John L. Lewis (1977), the Communists and the C.I.O. (1977), black workers and the UAW (1979), and the textile workers' struggle at Roanoke Rapids (1979).

THE UNIFYING LESSON

Perhaps, the unifying lesson implicit in the work of recent labor historians is that their subject not only touches on, but necessarily reshapes the way we look at the larger contours of American history. Herbert Gutman has pointed out that the essential subject matter of labor historians is sometimes mistakenly balkanized into labor history, mobility history, immigration history, women's history, family history, Black history, urban history, business history, religious history, and others. What we are really talking about is simply what is required "to study the people" who have composed the American industrial heritage. There is, perhaps, something more as well. Early in the 1960s, the cry went up from scholars like Jesse Lemisch (1968) and Staughton Lynd (1964) to study history "from the bottom up," an invocation which pointed to the importance of non-elite experience, not only as a matter of intellectual curiosity but as a means to revise our basic understanding of the nation's past. Lemisch (1968) and Alfred Young (1964) did this by focusing on the role of the artisans and other plebian groups in the era of the American Revolution. From a quite different vantage point, Stephan Thernstrom's study of working-class mobility (1964, 1973) also seeks to explain the peculiarities of American political culture through an understanding of the objective experience of the lower classes. David Montgomery's *Beyond Equality* (1967), which sets the labor question at the center of the republican tradition, likewise is as much a revision of political history as labor history. The past fifteen years of scholarship have, in short, seen a critical redefinition of issues of concern to labor historians. No doubt, the field has not seen the last of its internal "upheaval."

[5]See, E.G., Stanley Aronowitz, *False Promises: The Shaping of American Working Class Consciousness* (New York: McGraw-Hill, 1973); Ronald Radosh, "The Corporate Ideology of American Labor Leaders from Gompers to Hillman," *Studies on the Left* 6 (Nov.-Dec.. 1966): 66–88; Radosh, *American Labor and United States Foreign Policy* (New York: Random House, 1970); John Hutchinson, *The Imperfect Union; A History of Corruption in American Trade Unions* (New York: Dutton, 1970). Compare such works to, e.g., Melvyn Dubofsky, *We Shall Be All, A History of the Industrial Workers of the World* (Chicago: Quadrangle, 1969); Alice and Staughton Lynd, *Rank and File: Personal Histories By Working Class Organizers* (Boston: Beacon Press, 1973); and James J. Matles and James Higgins, *Them and Us: Struggles of a Rank-and-File Union* (Englewood Cliffs, N.J.: Prentice-Hall, 1974).

WORKS CITED

Benson, Susan Porter, "The Clerking Sisterhood," *Radical America* 12 (March-April 1978): 41–55.
Brody, David, *Steelworkers in America, The Non-Union Era*. Cambridge, Massachusetts: Harvard University Press, 1960.
_____, *Workers in Industrial America, Essays on the Twentieth Century Struggle*. New York: Oxford, 1980.
Cochran, Bert, *Labor and Communism: The Conflict That Shaped American Unions*. Princeton: Princeton University Press, 1977.
Conway, Mimi, *Rise Gonna Rise, A Portrait of Southern Textile Workers*. New York: Anchor, 1979.
Dawley, Alan, *Class and Community, The Industrial Revolution in Lynn*. Harvard Studies in Urban History. Cambridge, Massachusetts: Harvard University Press, 1976.
Dublin, Thomas, *Women at Work: The Transformation of Work and Community in Lowell, Massachusetts, 1826–1860*. New York: Columbia University Press, 1979.
Dubofsky, Melvyn and Van Tine, Warren, *John L. Lewis: A Biography*. New York: Quadrangle, 1977.
Edwards, Richard, *Contested Terrain, The Transformation of the Workplace in the Twentieth Century*. New York: Basic Books, 1979.
Faler, Paul, "Cultural Aspects of the Industrial Revolution: Lynn, Massachetts, Shoemakers and Industrial Morality, 1826–1860," *Labor History* 15 (Summer 1974): 367–394.
Friedlander, Peter, *The Emergence of a UAW Local, 1936–39, A Study in Class and Culture*. Pittsburgh: University of Pittsburgh Press, 1975.
Garlock, Jonathan and Builder, N.C., "Knights of Labor Data Bank: Users Manual and Index to Local Assemblies," unpublished ms., University of Rochester, 1973.
Green, James R., *The World of the Worker, Labor in Twentieth Century America*. New York: Hill and Wang, 1980.
Grob, Gerald, *Workers and Utopia, A Study of Ideological Conflict in the American Labor Movement 1865–1900*. Evanston: Northwestern University Press, 1961.
Gutman, Herbert G., *Work, Culture and Society in Industrializing America*. New York: Knopf, 1976. See especially, in chronological order, "Two Lockouts in Pennsylvania, 1873–1874" (1959); "Protestantism and the American Labor Movement: The Christian Spirit in the Gilded Age" (1966); "Class, Status, and Community Power in Nineteenth Century American Industrial Cities—Paterson, New Jersey: A Case Study" (1968); "The Negro and the United Mine Workers of America: The Career and Letters of Richard L. Davis and Something of Their Meaning, 1890–1900" (1968); and "Work, Culture, and Society in Industrializing America, 1815–1919" (1973).

———, *The Black Family in Slavery and Freedom, 1750-1925*. New York: Pantheon, 1976.
Kealey, Gregory S., *Toronto Workers Respond to Industrial Capitalism 1867-1892*. Toronto: University of Toronto Press, 1980.
Lemisch, Jesse, "The American Revolution Seen From the Bottom Up," in Barton J. Bernstein, ed., *Towards a New Past: Dissenting Essays in American History*. New York: Pantheon, 1968.
———, "Jack Tar in the Streets: Merchant Seamen in the Politics of Revolutionary America," *William and Mary Quarterly* 25 (July 1968): 371-407.
Lynd, Staughton, "The Mechanics in New York Politics," *Labor History* 5 (Fall 1964): 225-246.
Meier, August and Rudwick, Elliott, *Black Detroit and the Rise of the UAW*. New York: Oxford, 1979.
Montgomery, David, *Beyond Equality: Labor and the Radical Republicans 1862-1872*. New York: Knopf, 1967.
———, "The Shuttle and the Cross: Weavers and Artisans in the Kensington Riots of 1844," *Journal of Social History* 5 (Summer 1972): 411-46.
———, "The Working Classes of the Pre-Industrial American City, 1780-1830." *Labor History* 9 (Winter 1968): 3-22.
———, *Workers' Control in America, Studies in the History of Work, Technology, and Labor Struggles*. New York: Cambridge University Press, 1979.
Painter, Nell Irvin, *The Narrative of Hosea Hudson: His Life as a Negro Communist in the South*. Cambridge, Massachusetts: Harvard University Press, 1979.
Thernstrom, Stephan, *The Other Bostonians: Poverty and Progress in the American Metropolis, 1880-1970*. Cambridge, Massachusetts: Harvard University Press, 1979.
———, *Poverty and Progress, Social Mobility in a Nineteenth Century City*. Cambridge, Massachusetts: Harvard University Press, 1964.
Thompson, E. P., *The Making of the English Working Class*. New York: Pantheon, 1964.
Walkowitz, Daniel J., *Worker City, Company Town: Iron and Cotton Worker Protest in Troy and Cohoes, New York, 1855-84*. Urbana: University of Illinois, 1978.
Ware, Norman, *The Labor Movement in the United States, 1860-1895, A Study in Democracy*. New York: D. Appleton and Co., 1929.
Yans-McLaughlin, Virginia, *Family & Community: Italian Immigrants in Buffalo, 1880-1930*. Ithaca: Cornell University Press, 1977.
Young, Alfred, "The Mechanics and the Jeffersonians: New York, 1789-1801," *Labor History* 5 (Fall 1964): 247-76.

SUGGESTIONS FOR TEACHING ABOUT INDUSTRIAL AMERICA'S RANK AND FILE

The Transformation of the Working Place: Its Impact on the Shoemakers

FAY METCALF

As Leon Fink suggests in his chapter, the transformation of the working place has had a profound effect on the daily lives of American workers. If Alan Dawley's book is available, teachers will find it useful in preparing a background lecture for this lesson. However, the lesson may be used just as it appears as a simple example of the changes which industrialization forced upon individual workers.

TO THE STUDENT: In the following exercise, you will be reading accounts that describe the shoemaking industry at different times in American history. As you read the excerpts, keep these questions in mind:
1. What do these accounts of the shoemaking industry have in common? How are they different? Do they all reflect the bias of the writer?
2. The first account makes the domestic system appear to be a sort of "golden age" for the artisans. How would you find out if that were really so?
3. The two union organizers look upon the changes in the shoemaking industry from the point of view of the workers. In what ways would the perspective of the factory owners be different? How might consumers view the changes?
4. The last account was written in 1972. How would you find out the conditions in the shoemaking industry today? What changes would you anticipate had taken place?

Account #1: From Norman Ware, *The Industrial Worker, 1840–1860* (New York: Quadrangle Books, 1964), pp. 39–40.

In 1830 nearly all the shoemakers of Lynn (Massachusetts) had owned their homes with some land about them. . . . Almost every family kept a pig and many had their own cow. . . . With a garden, a pig, and some fishing tackle the shoemaker "could bid defiance to financial tempests." In the winter he could go clam and eel hunting, and if he had two or three cords of wood split and piled in the shed he considered himself in easy circumstances. . . .

The shoemaker had always been regarded as a thoughtful and intelligent artisan. Every shoeshop was a lyceum. It was a common thing for the journeymen to hire a boy to read the paper to them while they worked. . . . The shoemakers were distinguished for general intelligence. It was a social business, conversation was not drowned by the noise of machinery, and there were many opportunities for reading and mutual improvement.

Account #2: From the testimony of Horace M. Eaton, General Secretary-Treasurer of the Boot and Shoe Workers' Union, September 21, 1899, to the U.S. Congress, as reprinted in Leon Litwack, *The American Labor Movement* (Englewood Cliffs, N.J.: Prentice-Hall, 1962), pp.5–8.

Q. Taking the material as it is prepared for the shoemaker, how many hands does a gentleman's finished shoe pass through in the process of manufacture?
A. To answer that question in another way, there are about one hundred subdivisions of labor in the manufacture of a shoe. . . .
Q. Now, let me ask, in connection with that, what effect has that specializing . . . upon the workman? Has it a beneficial effect or otherwise?
A. Oh, it has been detrimental to the workman.
Q. The workman only knows how to perform the labor of one department?
A. That is all, and he becomes a mere machine. . . .
Q. What is the effect, generally speaking, of the employment of boys and girls in factories?
A. That is quite an evil. I have seen small children standing on boxes because they were not tall enough to stand up to a man's work and operate machines. . . . The introduction of child labor is quite a factor, sometimes displacing the head of the family. There was an instance. . . where a man was receiving $2 a day; the firm turned him off and put in his own son at $1, at the same job.

Account #3: From Studs Terkel, *Working* (New York: Pantheon Books, 1972), pp. 356–357.

JACK SPIEGEL

(He is an organizer for the United Shoe Workers of America.)
"About sixty percent in the industry are women. In some shops it goes as high as seventy percent. A great many are Spanish-speaking and blacks. It's low paying work. . . .

"Small shops are going out of business because they can't compete with the giants. There's been a lot of mergers in the shoe industry. Importation has cut into a third of the shoes being sold in our country. Shoes are brought in from Spain, Japan, Italy. . . . The average wage in this country is $2.60. In Italy it is $1.10.

"The same manufacturers who exploit here open up factories there, bring the shoes in here, finish 'em in some places, and put a 'Made in America' label on them. . . .

"Up to about twelve years ago, we had about a quarter of a million workers. There are now less than 170,000. In the next ten, fifteen years it may diminish to less than fifty thousand. . . .

"If some measures aren't taken by the government to tax those who send money out and establish those factories in other countries, and take jobs away from people here, it will be good-bye to the American shoe industry. Those in their sixties will retire. Those who are still able to work will find it more difficult."

Follow-Up: Discuss the reading questions with your classmates. List topics on which there is disagreement, and try to discover why such disagreement occurs. Select one of the questions which these excerpts raise in your mind and do research to discover an answer. Find other accounts of the shoemaking industry and compare them with these accounts. Check your textbook to see if that second-hand account leaves you with the same general impression of the changes in the shoemaking industry as these specialized versions do.

How the Transition from Household to Central Shop to Factory Methods of Production Affected Workers

CLAIR W. KELLER

This lesson presupposes that students learn history best when they engage in activities designed to use information that they have gathered from various sources to make some kind of product.[1] The following activity illustrates how students can explore changes in working life as production evolved from the household to the central shop and finally to the factory methods of production.

---

[1] For more on this idea, see Clair W. Keller, *Involving Students in the New Social Studies* (Boston: Little Brown, 1974), pp. 41–55.

Objectives: The student will be able to:

1. locate, gather, and relate data to a description of work during different methods of production.
2. describe how work involved in the making of different items changed during different methods of production.
3. compare and contrast how changes in work during different methods of production affected the lives of workers.
4. show the impact of technology on the lives of workers.
5. organize data to answer questions put forth in an imaginary (written) interview.

Procedures:

Acquiring and Organizing Data
1. Assign students to gather data on one of the following topics: household production of shoes,* furniture, soap,* dresses, candles,* nails, glass, or rifles*; or central shop production of shoes, furniture, soap, dresses, candles, nails, glass, or rifles; or factory production of shoes,* furniture, soap,* dresses, candles,* nails, glass, or rifles.* (*Suggested topics for less able students.) Gathering information for the central shop methods of production will be more difficult than for the other methods.
2. Students assigned to the same method of production — i.e., household — meet in a group to discuss the types of questions they should use in their investigation. (Providing students with a list of questions suggested by the retrieval chart [right] reduces the difficulty of the lesson.)
3. After gathering data on this topic, each student writes an imaginary interview with a worker who produces the item researched.[2] This is written in a question-answer format. (Having students cite sources of data increases the difficulty of the assignment.)

Application and Sharing of Data
4. Students again meet in groups composed of those who have gathered data for a particular method of production. These students share information and arrive at a general description of a worker's life during a particular method of production. (Providing students with a retrieval chart for summarizing findings reduces difficulty.)
5. Each group then reports its conclusions to the rest of the class. This can be done orally or in some written form. In any case, the teacher must develop a retrieval chart similar to the one at the right for easier summarization and comparison of data.

---

[2]For additonal uses of the interview, see Clair W. Keller, "Using Creative Interviews to Personalize Decisionmaking in the American Revolution," *Social Education* 43 (March, 1979), pp. 217–220.

INDUSTRIAL AMERICA'S RANK AND FILE

Retrieval Chart Comparing Methods of Production

Topic for Comparison	Household	Central Shop	Factory
Location of work			
Degree of specialization			
Number of persons engaged in producing item			
Number of persons at production site			
Type of energy used			
Type of tools used			
Degree of skill required of worker			
Type of skill needed			
Relative wage scale			
Type of worker			

Analysis and Debriefing Questions
1. What effect did the change in methods of production have on the worker?
2. Did the change in the method of production make work easier or harder?
3. At which method of production do you think working conditions were better?
4. What role did technology and energy play during each method of production?
5. Should all technological changes in work be encouraged?
6. What types of technological change do you foresee in the future?

Labor Unions/Organizations and the Community

D. L. SCHILLINGS

Whether in the city or on the farm, Americans today are profoundly affected by organized wage earners. With the growing trend to organize at almost all levels of society (from professional groups on one end of the spectrum to farm laborers on the other), such organizations and their membership are no longer restricted to our industrial centers and factory workers.

While most students see that organized wage earners have affected salaries, working conditions, volume of employment, and even quality of life, their understanding is generally based on the historical "has happened," and not on the present "is happening." Changing that perception is easier than might be assumed. There is a convenient, easily accessible source to show the impact of such organizations on today's society. Using their own community as a microcosm of America's labor force, students can be made aware of organized labor's impact. Questioning local citizens about their membership in, feelings about, and concerns with organized labor can provide the student with a sense of reality.

As simple as this approach might seem, it is often overlooked, perhaps because the teacher hesitates to involve the community in the learning process or feels unqualified to direct student questioning of community members. The following questionnaire should help to reduce those concerns. The categories and questions can certainly be adjusted to the individual teacher's desires, but the basic concerns of affiliation and attitude are applicable in all communities.

The end product will provide a point of departure for classroom discussions of what occupations are unionized, why people join unions, the benefits of membership, the problems which unions might create, and speculations about the size and impact of union membership. The teacher should be richly rewarded in the newly found interest that students bring to material that has suddenly become "real" to them. The added benefit of community involvement and awareness of what the classroom teacher is doing to help students understand the "real world" can pay dividends of community support that many teachers hope for, but seldom expect to receive.

Questionnaire for Studying Labor Unions/Organizations and the Community

To the Student:
1. Tell each person whom you interview *why* you are conducting this interview.
2. Be polite!
3. Ask the following questions in order.
4. After completing the interview, let the respondent see his or her answers, in order to make sure that you understood them correctly.
5. Thank the respondents for their time and assistance.

Respondent's Name:_____

Question #1: What is your occupation?_____

Question #2: Do you
   A. belong to a labor union?
   B. belong to a professional union or organization?
   C. belong to neither a labor union nor a professional union/organization?
   (If C is answered, skip to Question #5)

Question #3: What is the name of the labor union or professional union/organization to which you belong?
_____
   A. How long have you belonged?_____
   B. Do most people in your line of work belong to this union?
      Yes____   No____
      1. (If "Yes") Why?
      2. (If "No") Why not?   Why do you belong?

Question #4: Do you think belonging to this labor union or professional union/organization has been good for you? Why?

Question #5. (Non-union members only) Why don't you belong to a union?

Question #6. (Ask both union and non-union members this question.) What impact do you think unions have had on the American way of life? Has this been good or bad? Why?

BUREAU OF INDIAN AFFAIRS PHOTO

CHAPTER 5

Native American History: New Images and Ideas

LAWANA TROUT

To be an Indian in modern American society is in a very real sense to be unreal and ahistorical. . . . Experts paint Indians as they would like us to be. Often we paint ourselves as we wish we were or as we might have been. The more we try to be ourselves the more we are forced to defend what we have never been.
—*Vine Deloria, Jr.*

THE WRITING OF NATIVE AMERICAN HISTORY during the past two decades has been greatly influenced by the continuous turmoil in Native American affairs. Ethnologists, ecologists, industrialists, and government officials have all been riding off in different directions. Scarred by five centuries of physical and psychic upheavals, Native Americans themselves add to the chaos with tribal fights and factions. In the war of words, papers pile up, purging old guilt, but committing new sins. Historians stand at the center of this vortex, reevaluating the past and explaining the present. Since the sixties, Native Americans have insisted, "*Our* views of history will be heard," or as Deloria put it, "We talk, you listen!" In his sardonic bestseller, *Custer Died for Your Sins*, Deloria attacked stereotypes created by missionaries, anthropologists, and historians.* These negative images have influenced government policy and controlled public opinion. With *God Is Red, The Trail of Broken Treaties*, and *We Talk, You Listen*, Deloria composed a manifesto for the "new Indians" of the seventies. During that critical decade of civil and political strife, "red power" was used by militants to assert demands at the BIA Headquarters. In 1973, a national spotlight was trained on Wounded Knee when Russell Means told federal troops, "I'm going to die fighting for my treaty rights." In line with political agitation outside the

---

*For complete bibliographical information on the books mentioned in this chapter, see the bibliographical essay on pp. 101–103.

academy, scholars within began to include more Indians in accounts of American history, and the "New Indian History" was launched.

The single decade from 1970 to 1980 is richer in research on the political and cultural history of Native Americans than any other comparable period. While making important contributions to the historical literature, this scholarship has also uncovered a crucial question: What should be the nature of the new Indian history? The *new* must face the flaws of the *old*: the inaccurate images of mythic Indians, the inadequate analyses by historians and anthropologists, and the inevitable split between Native American and European views of history. The thrust of this chapter is to make clear the misuses of old images and the need for replacing them with more accurate ideas which will be less conducive to social and political manipulation.

The first aim of revisionist history is to remove bad images. The image game all started with Columbus, of course. (In Oklahoma, a popular bumper sticker quips, "Indians Discovered Columbus.") Believing his landing was in the Spice Islands, Columbus erred because his geography was faulty; nevertheless, his name for the people whom he saw stuck. That Euro-Americans labeled the Native Americans whom they encountered "the Indians" is in itself ridiculous. At least two thousand different cultures with a rich variety of beliefs and languages flourished in the Americas at the time of Columbus. Native Americans never formed a single culture, nor did they use a single term for themselves. Classifying these people as "Indians," Europeans grossly oversimplified native diversity, and the idea of *Indian* has perpetuated this misconception for five centuries.

Robert Berkhofer analyzes the widesweeping impact of the mythical "Indian" in *The White Man's Indian: Images of the American Indian from Columbus to the Present*. (Berkhofer makes a strong case for semantic distinction between *Indian* and *Native American*—the former designating a glass-case stereotype, the latter designating a living human being. Some historians prefer to keep and cleanse the term *Indian*. Since terminology fluctuates, this chapter includes both words within their historical contexts.) As Berkhofer unfolds the history of images through four centuries of religion, art, literature, and science, two sets of images are paramount. Native Americans are invariably presented as either good Indians or bad Indians, as either noble or ignoble savages. Whites have often changed their views to fit their needs, but the paradigm of polarity has remained constant.

The initial ambiguity, as Berkhofer illustrates, appeared in Columbus' letter of 1493. In favorable light, his natives were "handsome of stature," and "so guileless and generous with all they possess, that . . . they refuse nothing . . . and display as much love as if they give their hearts."[1] In contrast, Columbus also provided the first of the bad images: "a people who are regarded in all the islands as very fierce and who eat human flesh."[2] From this hearsay, but accurate, description of the Caribbean cannibals,

---

[1] Quoted in Robert F. Berkhofer, Jr., *The White Man's Indian: Images of the American Indian from Columbus to the Present* (New York: Vintage Books, 1978), p. 6.
[2] Quoted in *ibid.*, p. 7.

came the line of depraved savage images that were later erroneously associated with the original inhabitants of New England. The image of the savage Indian was highly useful to the English settlers. In 1625, Samuel Purchas noted that the savage natives did not "inhabit" their land: "On the other side, so good a Countrey, so bad a people . . . more brutish than the beasts they hunt, more wild and unmanly than that unmanned wild countrey, which they range [over] rather than inhabite."[3] Negative images were also useful for subsequent treaty negotiations. Two centuries later, Governor Gilmer of Georgia saw treaties as mere conveniences for taking land that the "savages" did not properly use. "Treaties were expedients by which ignorant, intractable, and savage people were induced without bloodshed to yield up what civilized people had the right to possess by virtue of that command of the Creator delivered to man upon his formation—be fruitful, multiply, and replenish the earth, and subdue it."[4] The "savage" Cherokee had signed these treaties, viewing them as supreme law of the land, and "civilized" citizens of the United States had signed, pledging their word and honor. Many tribes used treaties to reserve land for themselves, ensuring a land base for their own law, language, and culture. But some reformers in the late nineteenth century had as much faith in the magical effects of private property for civilizing Indians as some missionaries had in the miraculous influence of Christianity. Praising the moral values of private property, Merrill Gates, President of the Lake Mohawk Conference of the Friends of the Indian, resorted to the old stereotypes to make his point: "To bring him out of savagery into citizenship, we must make the Indian more intelligently selfish before we make him unselfishly intelligent. In his dull savagery, he must be touched by the wings of the divine angel of discontent . . . . Discontent is needed to get the Indian out of the blanket and into trousers—and trousers with a pocket in them, and with a *pocket that aches to be filled with dollars!*"[5] Gates pictured the Indian as "a little child" who had to learn his moral and economic lessons.

With these and more examples, Berkhofer rigorously documents how Whites created self-serving stereotypes which they used as ideological weapons in their subjugation of Native Americans. Unfortunately, the effects of these stereotypes are still multiplying. Past damage to Native American life is matched by present danger. Players of the name game are inventing new "rules and regs." One example is the debate over who is an Indian. The answer depends, in part, on who is asking and for what purpose. Most Native Americans respect cultural bonds of language, religion, and values. Federal policy arbitrarily sets a racial standard of one-quarter "Indian" blood as the minimum for receiving federal services. From Indians and non-Indians the labels flow: "acculturated/assimilated/annihilated," "real/unreal," "mixed blood/half-breed/full-blood." Bea Medicine, Lakota anthropologist, asks, "Does one set up a registry for 'Red bloods'?" Oklahoma artist Edgar Heap of

[3] Quoted in *ibid.*, p. 21.
[4] Quoted in *ibid.*, p. 161.
[5] Quoted in *ibid.*, p. 173.

Birds says, "Image-making is a form of social surgery to keep Native Americans legally crippled."

If *Indian* creates this confusion, what are we to do with Indian *history*? Again, we are on shifting ground. No single definition exists, and no one model holds. There are sharp splits among tribal traditionalists and academicians about the content and methodology of the new history which they all demand. The crux of the conflict rests in different cultural and historical traditions. Most Americans inherited a European tradition that defines history as a steady progression through time—an account carefully reconstructed from written documents, by experts committed to an ideal of scientific truth. For example, in "Doing Indian History," Francis Prucha writes, "History is a legitimate scholarly *discipline*, whose purpose is to reconstruct the past as accurately as the intelligence of the historian and the fullness of the historical sources permit . . . . It is a *scientific* study based on finely honed techniques."[6] (Italics added.) The science of historiography has been evolving for centuries; it is easy to see why academic architects of the new Indian history insist upon this approach.

In contrast, many Native Americans inherited oral historical traditions which emphasize metaphorical, rather than empirical, truth. This history respects the authority of old ones as keepers of tribal memory. Tribal historians aim to correct misinterpretations of their past and to preserve oral wisdom for future generations. They assert that birthright to a living culture gives their work a level of "truth" which outsiders cannot attain. For these traditionalists, sacred and secular events merge in cyclical time and sacred geography. America is a sacred land. Since human lives are linked to an animate universe, cosmos and state are not separate worlds. They insist that secular history without sacred (cosmic) history is only *half* the "truth." For example, it is impossible to appreciate the devastating effect of any removal treaty unless one recognizes the psychic scar that marks generations of Native Americans alienated from their homeland. It is impossible to understand the Lakotas' refusal to accept a court-decreed Black Hills settlement for one hundred and five million dollars unless one understands why some traditional Lakotas will never sell the sacred *Paha Sapa*. Albert White Hat, Rosebud tribal leader, relates the 1980 Black Hills Supreme Court decision to his identity as a Lakota:

O.K. This is what the lawyers told us, "Be realistic, there's no way you can get the land. It's already been sold." But you don't exchange money for mother earth; the minute we exchange monies for it, we're going to lose our identity. We're going to sell ourselves. I'll be a liar if I climb up on a hill and take up the pipe and pray to mother earth, because I exchange it with money. I don't want the money. If I accept that money, whether it's per capita or what, when I accept it, I hope I don't say I'm a Lakota. I'll accept it saying I'm a Catholic, Episcopal, or I'm a middle-class American. I'm an acculturated, assimilated Indian—but I'm not a Lakota![7]

---

[6]Francis Paul Prucha, "Doing Indian History," *Indian-White Relations: A Persistent Paradox*, Jane F. Smith and Robert Kvasnicka, eds. (Washington, D.C.: Howard University Press, 1976), pp. 1–10.
[7]Albert White Hat, Interview with Lawana Trout, July 29, 1980.

For Albert White Hat and other traditionalists, their new history must pay homage to both sacred and scientific icons.

There is another bitter contention between some tribal historians and many academicians. The European tradition uses distinct disciplines for interpreting cultures: history, anthropology, religion, philosophy, and literature, to name a few. Most historians honor the boundaries between these intellectual territories. Protecting their own turf, they often label oral-tradition genres "folk history," "quasi-religious stories," or "legendary tales"—legitimate literature, but illegitimate history. True to tribal training, many Native Americans see history as a cosmic-human circle, and they blame historians and anthropologists for fracturing this cycle. Deloria articulates their anger: "Into each life it is said some rain must fall . . . . But Indians have been cursed above all other people. Indians have anthropologists."[8] Had the tribes been given a choice of fighting the cavalry or anthropologists, Deloria continues, there is no doubt about their decision, for "anthros" threaten the existence of native people: "A warrior killed in battle could always go to the Happy Hunting Grounds. But where does an Indian laid low by an anthro go? To the Library?" Deloria also emphasizes the danger in false images perpetuated by anthros attempting to capture "real" Indians: "After all, who can conceive of a food-gathering, berry-picking, semi-nomadic, fire-worshiping, high-plains-and-mountain-dwelling, horse-riding, canoe-toting, bead-using, pottery-making, ribbon-coveting, wickiup-sheltered people . . . as real?"[9] Although Deloria's witty indictment of anthros and histos is not entirely accurate, other scholars have reached similar conclusions.

Berkhofer has criticized both history and anthropology on a number of grounds. In the first place, both have failed to face squarely the issue of continuity and change within native cultures. The paradox comes from two *seemingly* contradictory facts: traditional ways of life were changing drastically over the years, at the same time that personality traits and cultural patterns were supposedly remaining static. Anthropologists studied the aboriginal past and reservation present, while historians analyzed the period in between. Anthropologists collected data from informants, using contemporary information to describe past events. Historians went to the library, searching for books and manuscripts which placed an event in its chronological milieu. Even when the historian claimed to describe the Indian viewpoint, he or she rarely paid heed to the intertribal relationships. Therefore, historians often wrote history as a record of White-Indian relations. For historians, Whites were generally the major characters; for anthropologists, the Indian culture was the center of attention. Most damaging to accurate history was the presumption by both disciplines that Indians were a vanishing race. If the only good Indians were dead ones, the only lucky Indians were ones who lived in the past. Berkhofer concludes, "Indian history in this

---

[8]Vine Deloria, Jr., *Custer Died for Your Sins: An Indian Manifesto* (New York: Avon Books, 1969), p. 83.
[9]*Ibid.*, p. 87.

view moved implicitly, if not explicitly, in linear progression from noble or ignoble savage to reservation ward, to marginal man, and to eventual assimilation."[10]

The foregoing discussion suggests that the writing of Native American history has been bedeviled by false images, cultural clashes, and academic contrasts. With these problems in mind, we may now consider these questions: What are the differences in the ways traditional Native Americans and academics use the past, and what are the implications of these differences for writing new Indian history? Can the contributions of white ethno-historians combine with those of tribal historians to improve our knowledge of America's past, or are the two groups simply writing for different purposes and different audiences? Can—or should—tribal history become a part of United States national history? At this time, we have no adequate replies, but the debate continues; and some guidelines for a *different* history or histories are emerging: (1) Inter- and intra-tribal issues must be analyzed in addition to Indian-White relations. (2) Indian-White relations must be open to new interpretations. (3) Oral and written tribal history must be acknowledged as valid sources of Native American views. In short, American Indian history must change from being primarily a record of White-Indian relations to become the story of Native Americans in North America.

In his seminal essay, "The Political Context of the New Indian History," Berkhofer proposes that politics and power become the new focus or unifying center of Indian history. Using the broad definition of political behavior as encompassing conflict and resolution in religion, economics, politics, and culture, Berkhofer claims that emphasis on political behavior will highlight intertribal relations, will demonstrate that native cultures did not wither, and will extend the story's time span from pre-contact to urban present. Berkhofer also offers a simple checklist for analyzing any political context. What was the nature of the group's political organization? Who had the power? What processes produced the power? How was it used to affect cultural continuity and change? He also suggests that historians and anthropologists drop the fallacious idea that the tribe was always the basic unit.

The Indian *tribe* is an erroneous concept and image, created by Euro-Americans applying their own models to native cultures. In most cases, the tribe as a political entity developed after contact with white people. None of the so-called "tribes' originally used a governmental structure comparable to a state. The most common organization was a band comprised of small groups of families. The process of decision-making, adjudication, and implementation often extended beyond the family to the small band, but rarely to the entire group that Whites called "the tribe." Nor can scholars assume that native people moved in a certain sequence from band to tribe to chiefdom to state. Analysts must check the governmental taxonomy of any given group at a specific time in order to detect White perceptions and biases in historical

---

[10]Robert F. Berkhofer, Jr., "The Political Context of a New Indian History," *Pacific Historical Review*, XL (August 1971): 357-82.

documents and to find the real political machinery behind those "chiefs" and "kings" whom Whites often created.

Berkhofer also argues that analysts must be more sensitive to the role of factionalism in native affairs. Historians and anthropologists have paid little attention to the history of internal divisions. Many documents represent one side of a factional split, although they may have been misconstrued to represent the thinking of the whole group. Such one-sidedness colors and limits our understanding of how the leaders governed and who supported them in signing treaties and making other decisions. For example, we could understand what happened between the Whites and Cherokees better if we knew the full range of political behavior surrounding the Cherokee treaties of the 1830s; the whole issue of support for and opposition to removal is clouded by factional disputes.

The political view of Indian history is only one approach, but such a strategy does show Native Americans interacting with one another and coping with the world as they saw it. It does not reduce them to pawns in a chess game played by white people. Leaders are defined by their roles in the entire political process, rather than by a single criterion such as "patriot chief," "war chief," or "peace chief." Furthermore, the simple decline-and-death theme, so popular in previous Indian history, can be transformed into a more complex image of multiple declines and renascences.

The Death and Rebirth of the Seneca by Anthony F.C. Wallace meets all the criteria for a new Indian ethnohistory. Both historians and anthropologists welcomed his synthesis of sacred and secular history. The core of the story is the oral tradition of the Senecan prophet Handsome Lake. Handsome Lake grew to manhood and became an active hunter and warrior in an unvanquished Indian nation. The Seneca, most populous and most powerful of the confederated Iroquois tribes, guarded the doorway from which warriors traditionally issued to attack the western and southern nations, through which Iroquois hunters passed to exploit the conquered lands along the Allegheny and Ohio, and through which other nations, in friendship and war, had to travel before entering the home of the Iroquois. Intra-tribal politics are documented through Handsome Lake's quarrels with his brother Cornplanter and the powerful Red Jacket. The Senecas' internal troubles were aggravated by external pressures from Thomas Jefferson, the Quakers, and the blood feuds between the Seneca and other Iroquois nations. Wallace's book tells the story of how the Iroquois lived before the catastrophe hit them, the subsequent deterioration of tribal life, and how Handsome Lake and his disciples designed a new way to live and brought about a renaissance of Iroquois society.

As the title of Wallace's book implies, the Seneca were not a dying race. Today, one hundred and fifty years later, Handsome Lake's religion is still practiced on Iroquois reservations in the United States and Canada. The headquarters is on the Seneca Reservation at Tonawanda, New York (near Buffalo), where the wampum belts of Handsome Lake himself are kept—

belts so sacred that even the preachers may read them only once every two years, "on a sunny day when no fleece of cloud, even so big as a man's hand, can be seen in the sky." These preachers do not search through the old mildewed diaries and letters of the Quaker missionaries, nor do they compare differing versions of the tale of Handsome Lake in order to flesh out the bare bones of history. The holy ones intone what old men remembered their prophet having said to them, and "the sayings, hoarded like jewels in the memory, have been only a little polished as they passed from hand to hand."[11] Wallace has tied together the ends of time in his lyrical, yet logical, story of the Seneca past and present.

Scholars are shaping a new Indian history, discarding old images and discovering new ideas. Wallace has dispelled visions of a dying race; Berkhofer has described the impact of images on politics; and Deloria has poked holes in old myths. Francis Jennings has also challenged "old history," as written by Francis Parkman and his contemporaries. Jennings compared original sources with Parkman's story and found "matters of historical fact about which Parkman and others like him had been willfully and consistently misleading . . . so I set myself the task of unearthing the history that Parkman *et al.* had buried under an ideology. . . ."[12] In his revisionist history, Jennings has also pulverized familiar Puritan and Indian images, typified by the cardboard cutouts that decorate classroom walls each Thanksgiving.

In Jennings' *The Invasion of America: Indians, Colonialism, and the Cant of Conquest*, those who considered themselves the *real*, righteous, God-fearing folk play the "deed game" to gain illicit power and to steal Indian land. Replacing false images with fertile metaphors, Jennings has stripped away the religious rhetoric to reveal the cant of conquest. The land was more like a widow than a virgin. Euro-Americans did not settle a wilderness; they displaced a resident people. Europeans did not discover America. They invaded it. How could these invaders justify their mission of piety and plunder in the eyes of the world? Convinced that one man with God is a majority, the Puritans redeemed—and deceived—themselves with antithetical absolutes of "savagery" and "civilization." The basic myth of conquest postulates that the savages of the wilderness were incapable of civilizations, that the ennobled bearers of civilization were ordained by divine sanction to make the wilderness a garden, that the savages viciously resisted God or fate and thereby invited their suicidal extermination, and that it was all *inevitable*. Jennings deserves the historian's Oscar for his reevaluation of conquest ideology and his denial of the premise that all Indian-White contacts were created equal: "What Was in the Beginning has never again been quite the same."[13] Colonial Indian-White relations will never again be interpreted the same way after Jennings' brilliant exposé of colonial conquest of Indian land.

---

[11] Anthony F.C. Wallace, *The Death and Rebirth of the Seneca* (New York: Alfred A. Knopf, 1970), p. 10.
[12] Francis Jennings, *The Invasion of America: Indians, Colonialism, and the Cant of Conquest* (New York: W.W. Norton & Company, 1976), p. 42.
[13] *Ibid.*

Land has always been the center of legal and spiritual conflicts between Native Americans and Euro-Americans. With a more judicial eye, ethnohistorians are discarding old premises and reevaluating notes and other documents. Wilcomb Washburn's *Red Man's Land, White Man's Law* is a model survey of the land/law clashes. He shows that the Europeans acquired native land through European religious and secular law. Native Americans might have understood Christianity as preached on the shore of Galilee to the poor and oppressed, but Columbus the Christbearer (as his name and mission imply) carried an aggressive religion to the shore of the "new world." If the natives did not acknowledge the authority of this militant Church, they suffered dire consequences. The alternative, as stated in the "requirement," was read to Indians in order to legalize Spanish policy: "I certify to you that, with the help of God, we shall forcibly enter into your country and shall make war against you . . . and shall subject you to the yoke and obedience of the Church. . . . We shall take you and your wives and your children, and shall make slaves of them . . . and we shall take away your goods . . . and we protest that the deaths and losses which shall accrue from this are your fault."[14] The historian and apostle to the Indians, Bartolomé de las Casas, on reading the *Requerimiento*, could not decide whether to laugh or weep. Under the banner of God, Glory, and Gold, the Church made war itself an act of charity, killing or saving the natives. In either case, Euro-Americans gained the land.

Washburn dramatically documents how the law fell mercilessly upon native peoples for centuries; the words changed, but the policy did not alter. In 1793 Thomas Jefferson recognized the legal right of Indian nations to sell their lands *when they wished to sell*, and recognized that the "right of preemption," which replaced the "right of discovery," gave "no right of soil against the native possessors." In other words, the Indians had "full, undivided and independent sovereignty as long as they choose to keep it, and that this might be forever."[15] Forever in this case lasted less than forty years, until a conflict arose over Cherokee land between Chief Justice John Marshall and President Andrew Jackson. On Marshall's decision for Cherokee removal hinged the sanctity of treaty rights, the independence of numerous Indian nations, and even the very title of the real estate of the United States. The Cherokee lost not to the court, but to Jackson's refusal to enforce the Supreme Court's decision. Marshall, in deep gloom, wrote in 1832, "I yield slowly and reluctantly to the conviction that our constitution cannot last."[16]

The Constitution did last, and in 1887 there was another law affecting Indian land, the Dawes Severalty Act. This act had the backing of those who wished the Indians well and of those who wished them ill. About the only people who were not enthusiastic for the bill were those it was designed to help: the Indians. The catastrophic consequences of the severalty policy

---

[14]Quoted in Wilcomb E. Washburn, *Red Man's Land/White Man's Law: A Study of the Past and Present Status of the American Indian* (New York: Charles Scribner's Sons, 1971), p. 7.
[15]*Ibid.*, p. 56.
[16]Quoted in *ibid.*, p. 69.

appear in these astonishing figures: of the 138,000,000 acres of tribal landholdings in 1887, only 48,000,000 remained in 1934, the year of the Indian New Deal, or the Indian Reorganization Act. A way of life and a value system were destroyed as the natives' land base dwindled. Then, after the flush of victory following World War II, Congress enacted a new law to right old wrongs and to wipe the slate clean. The Indian Claims Commission came one hundred years too late for the Cherokees and millions of other Native Americans, but at last, for the first time, their descendents could bring land claims against the government without a special act of Congress.

We have seen that ethnohistorians are radically revising American history. Native Americans are also writing their own tribal histories. *Noon Nee-Mee-Poo (We, the Nez Percé)* by Allen Slickpoo is a personal, sometimes angry account of the way in which Nez Percé remember and interpret their past. In this book, "we, the Nez Percé" write a consensus history through a native son. Oral history gives a glimpse of private lives. One story is about Wet-khoo-weis, the first Nez Percé woman to see white people. In the eighteenth century, the Blackfeet captured her and took her to Canada. There she was sold to the Assiniboines and eventually purchased by a white man. His people treated her kindly, giving her medicine for trachoma, which raged among the Nez Percé. After giving birth to a child, she ran away, and during her wanderings, the child died. When Lewis and Clark arrived in 1805, this woman persuaded the Nez Percé not to kill their white visitors.

In addition to oral history, Slickpoo includes written sources such as treaty proceedings. Writing from the Nez Percé perspective, he tells how his people lost their physical and spiritual homeland. He also comments that both Indians and Whites were probably speaking *past* rather than *to* each other because of the language barriers. Nevertheless, both groups believed that they spoke "from the heart." Owhi united land, heart, and spirit: "It is the earth that is our parent . . . God named this land to us. Shall I steal this land and sell it? This is the reason my heart is sad. My friends, God made our bodies from the earth."[17] General Palmer did not call the earth his mother, but he called the Nez Percé "my brothers" and cajoled them to sign the treaty. "I too love the earth where I was born. . . . You people have sometimes done wrong. Our hearts have cried. Our hearts still cry, but if you will do right, we will forget it."[18] ("Do right" meant "sign the treaty.") When all signatures were at last given, General Palmer made promises: "We came here to talk straight, we have shown you our hearts. We will not lie to you. We expect you to leave this ground with good hearts and if there are any among you that have bad hearts, advise them to throw them away." The General also assured the Nez Percé, "We buy your country and pay you for it and give the most of it back to you again."[19]

[17] Allen P. Slickpoo, Sr., *Noon Nee-Me-Poo (We, the Nez Percé)* (The Nez Percé Tribe of Idaho, 1973), p. 120.
[18] Quoted in *ibid.*, p. 121.
[19] Quoted in *ibid.*, p. 134.

Miners found gold, and all hearts changed. Chief Joseph's band refused to sign "the steal treaty" for relinquishing more land. Joseph led the rebels in the 1877 War until he surrendered to General Miles. With historical irony, "heart" appeared in the tragedy. Joseph handed his rifle to General Miles and said, "Tell General Howard I know what is in his heart. What he told me before, I have in my heart. . . . It is cold and we have no blankets. The little children are freezing . . . I want to have time to look for my children and see how many of them I can find. Maybe I shall find them among the dead."[20]

Slickpoo's chronicle of the Nez Percé sparked hot words between academics and tribalists at a session of the American Historical Association on the writing of Indian history. Academics criticized Slickpoo's failure to use footnotes and to follow standard documentary form. Some found fault with the book's lack of objectivity, calling it "the type of history which assuages wounded Native American ego." Slickpoo and the Nez Percé elders undoubtedly expected this criticism, for they had written in the text: "We have listed a bibliography of the written sources we have consulted, but we do not always cite them in footnotes. It is our culture and history and we do not have to prove it to anyone by footnoting."[21] Slickpoo concludes, "Our history in many instances has become alienated from us by the 'Indian experts' who are coming in greater numbers than the American Indians themselves."[22]

Both Deloria and Slickpoo distrust alien experts. Their skepticism is natural, since outsiders testify in land claims, formulate laws, and administer policy. These experts use documents from "official history," and too often jobs disappear, Indian schools close, and cultural projects die. Therefore, history is not an academic exercise about the past; history is the present for Native Americans. The future depends on ethnohistorians' reevaluating old images and providing new ideas. Tribal historians who are secure both in the academic world and the tribal world must play a larger role, sensitive to written records and to oral traditions of their own people. The seventies laid the foundation for a more authentic Indian history. The eighties should mark its evolution. By the nineties, a new Indian history could exist, and this history could create a new existence for Native Americans.

BIBLIOGRAPHY

If we imagine these titles as books on a reference shelf, the first must be Prucha, Francis P., *A Bibliographical Guide to the History of Indian-White Relations in the United States* (Chicago: University of Chicago Press, 1977). The topics, comments, and 9,705 entries of this "encyclopaedia" generate new ideas for reading and teaching. Complements to Prucha's volume are

---
[20]Quoted in *ibid.*, p. 193.
[21]*Ibid.*, p. viii.
[22]*Ibid.*, p. 279.

Jennings, Francis, ed., *The Newberry Library Center for the History of the American Indian Bibliographical Series* (Bloomington: Indiana University Press). Each volume includes an essay plus a list of works for a basic library collection on that subject. In addition, four articles survey scholarship from 1950-1978: Washburn, Wilcomb, "The Writing of American Indian History: A Status Report," *Pacific Historical Review* XL (August 1971): 261-82; Edmunds, David R., "The Indian in the Mainstream: Indian Historiography for Teachers of American History Surveys," *History Teacher* 8 (February 1975): 242-264; Prucha, Francis P., "Books on American Indian Policy: A Half-Decade of Important Work, 1970-75," *The Journal of American History* LXIII (December 1976): 658-669; and Axtell, James, "The Ethnohistory of Early America: A Review Essay," *William and Mary Quarterly*, 3rd. Ser., 35 (January 1978): 110-144.

In the category of new general histories, an indispensable set is Sturtevant, William C., ed., *Handbook of North American Indians* (Washington, D.C.: U.S. Government Printing Office). Of the projected twenty volumes, three are available: *California, Southwest,* and *Northeast.* Two additional surveys of cultural areas are Hudson, Charles, *The Southeastern Indians* (Knoxville: University of Tennessee Press, 1976) and Spicer, Edward H., *Cycles of Conquest: The Impact of Spain, Mexico, and the United States on the Indians of the Southwest, 1533-1960* (Tucson: University of Arizona Press, 1962). Other major surveys include Debo, Angie, *A History of the Indians of the United States* (Norman: University of Oklahoma Press, 1970); McNickle, D'Arcy, *The Indian Tribes of the United States* (New York: Oxford University Press, 1961): Spicer, Edward H., *A Short History of the Indians of the United States* (New York: Van Nostrand, 1969); and Washburn, Wilcomb, *The Indian in America* (New York: Harper and Row, 1975). The best general histories of Indian leaders are Edmunds, David, ed., *American Indian Leaders, Studies in Diversity* (Lincoln: University of Nebraska Press, 1980) and Josephy, Alvin M., Jr., *The Patriot Chiefs: A Chronicle of Indian Resistance* (New York: Viking Press, 1961). Two general volumes for the mass market are well illustrated: Maxwell, James, ed., *America's Fascinating Indian Heritage* (Pleasantville: Reader's Digest Association, 1978) and *The World of the American Indian* (New York: National Geographic Society, 1979).

A valuable reference for early America is Crosby, Alfred E., *The Columbian Exchange* (Westport: Greenwood Publishing Corporation, 1971), which documents the impact of contact upon both Old and New Worlds. In "Indian-White Relations in Early America: A Review Essay," Bernard Sheehan argues that historians cannot use modern standards to condemn America's past Indian policies, *William and Mary Quarterly* XXVI (April 1969): 267-86. These books examine such policies: Graymont, Barbara, *The Iroquois in the American Revolution* (Syracuse: University of Syracuse Press, 1972); and Leach, D.E., *Flintlock and Tomahawk: New England in King Philip's War* (New York: Macmillan, 1958). Two other books look at colonial history from a new perspective: Nash, Gary B., *Red, White and Black: The Peoples of Early America* (Englewood Cliffs, N.J.: Prentice-Hall, 1974) and Axtell, James, *The Indian Peoples of Eastern America: A Documentary History of the Sexes* (New York: Oxford University Press, 1981).

A multitude of books deal with nineteenth-century policy, including these notable ones: Prucha, Francis, *American Indian Policy in the Formative Years* (Cambridge: Harvard University Press, 1962); Satz, Ronald, *American Indian Policy in the Jacksonian Era* (Lincoln: University of Nebraska Press, 1975); Sheehan, Bernard, *Seeds of Destruction: Jeffersonian Philosophy and the American Indian* (Chapel Hill: University of North Carolina Press, 1973); Trennert, Robert A., *Alternative to Extinction: Federal Indian Policy and the Beginnings of the Reservation System, 1846-51* (Philadelphia: Temple University Press, 1975); Utley, Robert, *Frontier Regulars: The United States Army and the Indian, 1866-1891* (New York: Macmillan, 1973); Washburn, Wilcomb, *The Assault on Indian Tribalism: The General Allotment Law (Dawes Act) of 1887* (Philadelphia: J.B. Lippincott, 1975); and Wilkins, Thurman, *Cherokee Tragedy: The Story of the Ridge Family and the Decimation of a People* (New York: Macmillan, 1970). Historical writing on twentieth-century affairs appears primarily in journals (see citations in companion essays and above bibliographies). One major work is Hertzberg, Hazel, *The Search for an American Indian Identity: Modern Pan-Indian Movements* (Syracuse: University of Syracuse Press, 1971). The best interdisciplinary periodical for contemporary issues is *American Indian Culture and Research Journal* (American Indian Studies Center, University of California).

SUGGESTIONS FOR TEACHING NATIVE AMERICAN HISTORY

Teaching Native American History: Three Approaches

LAWANA TROUT

With rare exceptions, Native American history is not taught in secondary classrooms. It is an indisputable and startling fact that most high school teachers omit Native American tribal history and distort the history of Indian-White relations. These teachers do not deliberately ignore Native American history; they are simply unaware of its existence. Secondary texts are equally unreliable. Extraneous notes on Native Americans are tucked in with material about the landing of the Pilgrims and the winning of the West.

In walk-on roles, Pocahantas saves John Smith, Chief Joseph surrenders, and Geronimo goes to the Ft. Sill prison. In these texts, Indians do not speak from treaty proceedings or in tribal meetings. After analyzing a wide range of history textbooks in 1965, Indian scholars made this indictment: "Our examination discloses that not one book is free from error as to the role of the Indian in state and national history. We Indians believe everyone has the right to his opinion. A person also has the right to be wrong. But a textbook has no right to be wrong, or to lie, hide the truth, or insult and malign a whole race of people. That is what these textbooks do."[1] The texts of the 1980s have a new look. There are photographs of Red Cloud and Sitting Bull along with quotes from Black Hawk and Crazy Horse, but the revisions are cosmetic. Catlin's portraits and Curtis' photographs appear, but where are illustrations from fine Native American artists such as Mopope and Tiger? Inadequate texts and unaware teachers perpetuate a cycle of cultural blindness. Today, teachers may break this cycle by bridging the gap between scholarship and their classrooms. In this part of this Bulletin, I will give brief working notes for units on images, policy, and autobiography which integrate scholarship and strategy.

The unit "Native American Images" unfolds in three stages. Students are asked (1) to recognize and record negative and positive images, (2) to study the history of images and their influence on policy, and (3) to investigate for an independent project. In the first section, the class examines biased images in words, pictures, and films. Students begin by exploring the idea that *a word is a feeling*. These simple exercises may be springboards for students to create their own examples; defending their choices will help them to realize the influence of "loaded" words in various situations. Students compare these paired items: (1) finest quality filet mignon/first-class piece of dead cow, (2) Cubs trounce Giants 11-5/Score—Cubs 11, Giants 5, (3) "The only good Indian is a dead Indian"/"Indians are a vanishing race." They are asked to rank these words and phrases from positive to negative: (1) obscene film, nasty movie, shocking cinema, lewd movie, an honest and brave flick, pornographic show; (2) dame, woman, babe, lady, floozie, chick, miss, female, belle. Other lists might include males, adolescents, Blacks, Indians, and names of other groups. After playing with the words, students may discuss the differences in connotations and denotations.

Each word has its own "personality," and each picture is visual history. What happens when words are combined with pictures to manipulate opinions? *Indian Kitch: The Use and Misuse of Indian Images* is a collection of visuals used for propaganda and profit. On a random odyssey across America, Fritz Scholder photographed absurd transformations of "the Indian image." In his photographs, fantasy Indians appear as freaks and fakes: a life-size wooden statue stands in a curio store; a giant Katchina advertises "DRINK WITH REAL INDIANS"; and blinking kewpie dolls pressed from

---
[1]Rupert Costo, *Textbooks and the American Indian* (San Francisco: The Indian Historian Press, Inc., 1970), p. 7.

plastic appear in roadside stops along Route 66. Says Scholder, "From belt buckles to billboards, the Indian is in. But is in only for income?" Tourists still buy an object as long as it is made by Indians, but the paint is peeling from wooden wigwams; and signs such as "100% INDIAN" and "HURRY BACK!" have weeds and empty cans as companions. The cement tepees, neon arrows, and trading-post gimmicks are endless. Scholder concludes, "In the beginning, it was the Indian who was exploited; later even the Indian would dilute the Indian. . . . This mass media society has overkilled the American Indian more than once. What is left is a factoid of the fact."[2] It is dangerous to reinforce negative images without providing positive ones. Classes must browse through scores of art and photography books such as *Song from the Earth: American Indian Painting* by Jamake Highwater. *Native Americans: 500 Years After* is a unique photographic collage of real people: a Tesuque pueblo team playing baseball; a young Laguna woman wearing native dress; and Kiowas, Apaches, and Comanches dancing and drumming at a pow-wow. *Indians, The First Americans* is an impressive set of photographs of many subjects, ranging from Red Horse's ledger drawing of the Battle of the Little Big Horn to the protest takeover of the BIA in 1972. In discussing these and other collections, students may treat each photograph as a historical document. What does the camera eye see? What is the picture's purpose? Who is the audience? What probably existed beyond the edge of the frame? What other picture might have been taken of the same subject from a different point of view? If a single photograph is a historical moment, a series of photographs is a historical drama. *Home of the Brave*, a short, non-dialogue film, documents the Indian-White struggle for the West through a photo montage. I ask students to adopt a specific viewpoint—White, Indian, or neutral—as they watch the flashing symbols. Later, we discuss their divergent interpretations of the cinematic message.

After detecting bias in words, pictures, and films, students are able to record the uses and misuses of Indian images in their own lives. Questions may guide their study: What are the most common images around you? How are they used? How do you think that Native Americans would react to them? Images may be collected from billboards, television programs, books, periodicals, and daily newspapers. Students may take an opinion poll by asking ten people at random, "What do you see when I say *Indian? Native American?*" Comparing surveys, the class may make an image profile. What does the profile say about Native Americans? The informants? Speculations about the origins of these images will introduce the second stage of the study: a history of images.

Hugh Honour's *The New Golden Land: European Images of America from Discoveries to the Present Time* and Robert Berkhofer's *The White Man's Indian* are the best sources for students to use in analyzing the history of images and their influence on policy. A section of either text may be a mini-study. For example, all students know the western formulas which

[2] Fritz Scholder, *Indian Kitsch* (Flagstaff: Northland Press, 1979), Introduction.

place stock characters in predictable plots and settings. In his section "The Western and the Indian in Popular Culture," Berkhofer shows that modern media Indians are composite figures that have evolved from characters in captivity narratives, Cooper's *Leatherstocking Tales*, Buffalo Bill's Wild West Show, dime novels, programs involving Tonto and "The Lone Ranger," and, finally, "B" Western movies. Today, the Western as timeless epic has been ironically flipped to become pop culture. Arthur Penn's *Little Big Man*, Robert Altman's *Buffalo Bill and the Indians, or Sitting Bull's History Lesson*, and other anti-establishment Westerns are examples of celluloid counter-culture. Students interested in this topic may consult Gretchen M. Bataille's *The Pretend Indians: Images of Native Americans in Movies*. For example, many teenagers idolize the character Billy Jack. In his Foreword, Deloria comments, "Consider the movie *Billy Jack*, better titled 'Bully Jack.' Bully Jack is a pacifist who demonstrates his commitment to nonviolence by riding around an obscure western Indian reservation and breaking people's necks."

The Pretend Indians is also an excellent source for students' independent projects in section three of the unit. Previous activities have prepared them to apply their insights to more complex investigations. For example, they may analyze the image of the "old chief" in movies and literature. This weathered veteran appears in the book and movie *Little Big Man*, Carlos Castaneda's Yaqui Don Juan series, *Hanta Yo*, and literally thousands of books, photographs, movies, posters, and other media. Another class project may focus on the film series *Images of Indians*, which surveys the impact of the 2000 "cowboy and Indian" films produced since 1913.

In their campaign to replace static stereotypes with accurate ethnographic details, students may test their textbooks as another project. Adolescents know that they learn little history from texts, but they do not know the deliberate bias of editors and publishers who try to please the mass market. *America Revised*, by Frances FitzGerald, and *Stereotypes, Distortions and Omissions in U.S. History Textbooks*, published by the Council for Interracial Books for Children, are excellent guides for detecting such bias. Students must closely analyze style, content, and illustrations as they rate their text on twenty-six points relating to land, values, and images. When the class has rated a segment, each student may rewrite a brief passage. Then the writers test their private bias on one another as they gradually revise the entire text to eliminate ethnocentricism.

The image of the mystic warrior of the plains has eclipsed the real history of many Native Americans, particularly the Sioux, who say, "A people without history is like wind on the buffalo grass." The Sioux have history, but it is invisible to most Americans. "The Fort Laramie Treaty of 1868: Past and Present"* is a policy unit which traces the historical consequences of this

---

*Space permits only a cursory outline of this unit, edited by Jerry Boevers in a curriculum project sponsored by The Newberry Library and the National Endowment for the Humanities. For additional information, write to The Center for the History of the American Indian, The Newberry Library, 60 West Walton Street, Chicago, IL 60610.

treaty for the United States and for the Sioux Nation. In this study, students review the treaty-making process as one type of solution to the legal and spiritual clashes between Euro-Americans and Native Americans involving land, law, and culture. The 1868 Laramie Treaty is a historical magnet, attracting a chain of linked events: the 1973 siege of Wounded Knee, the 1890 massacre at Wounded Knee, the Battle of the Little Big Horn, and the 100-year battle for the Black Hills.[3] In unraveling the treaty story, students first ask, "What happened at Wounded Knee in 1973?" Some answers are in *Voices from Wounded Knee*. It began when the militants presented a proclamation to abolish the tribal government: "Let it be known this day, March 11, 1973, that the Oglala Sioux people will revive the treaty of 1868 and that . . . we are a sovereign nation by the treaty of 1868."[4] Russell Means, AIM leader, told the federal troops, "You're going to have to kill us. Because I'm not going to die in a barroom brawl. I'm not going to die when I walk into Pine Ridge, and Dickie's goons feel I should be offed. I'm going to die fighting for my treaty rights."[5] After 70 days, the siege ended, and the treaty war moved from the small Oglala village to a Lincoln, Nebraska, courtroom. Students may trace this trial by reading *The Great Sioux Nation*, a collection of testimony from witnesses, including Leonard Crow Dog, Sioux spiritual leader; Vine Deloria, one of the case attorneys; and Roxanne Ortiz, editor of the text. In this landmark case, for the first time, the *oral history* of the treaty was admitted as evidence. This oral history documents the years from 1850–1890 when white miners, soldiers, missionaries, and government officials clashed with Red Cloud, Sitting Bull, Crazy Horse, and their people. Students may read the written history in sources such as Robert Utley's *The Last Days of the Sioux Nation*, Mari Sandoz's *Crazy Horse*, Stanley Vestal's *Sitting Bull*, and Richard Erdoes' *The Sun Dance People*. Lone Dog's Winter Count is a Sioux Calendar of the years 1801–1870. After becoming familiar with Red Cloud's War, the Fetterman Massacre, and other events along the bloody Bozeman trail, students may draft their own treaties. Role-playing the divergent points of view in a simulation treaty council will help the treaty-makers to realize the moral and legal dilemmas in the negotiations which whittled away Sioux land and confined them to the reservation.

In the next stage of the unit, the class members analyze the 1868 Treaty, comparing it with their own efforts. Two excellent sources for this analysis are *Treaties and Agreements and the Proceedings of the Treaties and Agreements of the Sioux Nation* and Nick Meinhardt's "Reviewing U.S. Treaty Commitments to the Lakota Nation," *American Indian Journal* (January, 1978). The Ft. Laramie signatures were scarcely set when things began to fall apart. In 1874, George Custer led an illegal expedition into the Black

---

[3]For other treaty studies, see Donald Worcester, ed., *Forked Tongues and Broken Treaties* (Caldwell: Caxton Printers, 1975); Vine Deloria, *Behind the Trail of Broken Treaties* (New York: Dell, 1974); Kirke Kickingbird, *Indian Treaties* (Washington, D.C.: Institute for the Development of Indian Law, 1980); and Kirke Kickingbird, *One Hundred Million Acres* (New York: Macmillan, 1973).
[4]Robert Anderson, ed., *Voices from Wounded Knee*, 1973 (Rooseveltown: Akwesasne Notes, 1974), p. 55.
[5]*Ibid.*, p. 136.

Hills, found gold, and set in motion the events that would leave him dead upon the hill near the Little Big Horn in less than two years. More words have been written about this battle perhaps than any other in American history. Sifting through rich piles of fact and fiction, students may collect evidence for a trial centering on the actions of Reno, Benteen, and Custer. Important sources include *The Warrior Who Killed Custer; Custer's Last Stand*, by Robert Utley; and *The Battle of the Little Big Horn*, by Mari Sandoz. The United States Army lost George Custer in 1876, and the Sioux lost the Black Hills in 1877. Other losses of land and lives have never been forgotten. By New Year's Day 1890, Crazy Horse was dead, Sitting Bull was dead, United States soldiers were dead, and the frozen bodies of the Ghostdancers lay on the Wounded Knee battlefield. Students may read accounts of these tragedies in *Black Elk Speaks* and Dee Brown's *Bury My Heart at Wounded Knee*. But the Sioux Nation and the Ft. Laramie Treaty did not die. One hundred years after Custer's expedition, the Indian Claims Commission found that the United States had violated the treaty in taking the Black Hills. Students may watch the Black Hills case entering the Court of Claims in 1923 and emerging in the Supreme Court Decision of 1980. Some Sioux refused to accept the money: Elijah Whirlwind Horse announced, "The Oglala Tribal Council has taken the official position that the sacred Black Hills are not for sale." New disputes are arising among the Sioux and between the tribal governments and the United States courts. As students collect evidence representing different viewpoints, they may prepare another dramatic classroom trial: *The Sioux Nation* vs. *The United States*. As they complete this unit on land, law, and culture, classes will understand why the Sioux believe today that the Ft. Laramie Treaty is *living* history.

History meets autobiography in the third unit, "I Am History." Students have seen that legal words are pressed into service in battles over land in the "Laramie" study and that biased words carry racial scars in the "Images" analysis. Words create a common bond between Native American and other ethnic experiences as classes read and discuss vivid passages from Native American autobiographies and then write about similar feelings and happenings in their lives.[6] The trick is to limit the words to blood-and-bones autobiography. Writers may eliminate the excess fat through this simple process: (1) identifying the strong images (word pictures) in the model; (2) talking to themselves on paper, allowing thoughts to flow freely, without concern for grammar or structure; and (3) editing their work for accuracy and lean details.

Native American passages must match motifs in students' lives. For example, we all recall and relive scenes from childhood. Pretty Shield, Crow Medicine woman recalls in *Pretty Shield*, "My oldest sister had made me a

---

[6]See, for example, Arlene B. Hirschfelder, *American Indian and Eskimo Authors* (New York: Association on American Indian Affairs, 1973); Donald Jackson, ed., *Black Hawk: An Autobiography* (Urbana: University of Illinois Press, 1974); Peter Nabokov, ed., *Native American Testimony* (New York: Thomas Crowell, 1978); and A. L. Stensland, *Literature by and about the American Indian* (Urbana: National Council of Teachers of English, 1973).

kicking-ball. The thin skin that is over a buffalo's heart is taken off and stuffed with antelope hair. My ball was a very fine one, painted red and blue."[7] Helen Sekaquaptewa had a sad memory of being forced to leave her Hopi family in 1906 for a boarding school. "We now were loaded into wagons driven by our enemies. . . . We were taken to the schoolhouse in New Oraibi, with military escort. Evenings we would gather in a corner and cry softly so the matron would not hear and scold or spank us."[8] In 1968, Belle Frances, Athabascan, also left her reservation home. "Here I am in a big city, right in the middle of Chicago. I don't know anybody. I am so lonesome. . . . I see strange faces around me. . . . I know I have to overcome the fear I am holding inside me."[9] Students, too, must cope with the trauma of leaving loved ones, moving to a new home, or attending a different school. It may be necessary to suggest an opening line to unlock their thoughts: "I walked into the strange classroom and everyone stared at me."

At times, all adolescents consciously reach for adulthood. In his quest for vision, John Lame Deer looked for his future self. Alone and afraid on a hilltop, he held the peace pipe for courage: "As I ran my fingers along its bowl of smooth red pipestone, red like the blood of my people, I no longer felt scared."[10] Lame Deer longed to be a healer in the ancient ways, like the medicine men in his family who had chosen that spot for meditation for 200 years; their spirits were near: "I thought I could sense their presence right through the earth I was leaning against. I could feel them entering my body, feel them stirring in mind and heart. Then I felt the power surge through me like a flood. . . . I would become a wicasa wakan, a medicine man. . . . I wept with happiness."[11]

Like Lame Deer, most people share experiences that bind together their generations. Students may use *Navajo Stories of the Long Walk Period* as a model for collecting oral history. Chahadineli Benally tells of his grandmother who was expecting a child when she was captured by the Mexicans. She escaped, and, on her hard journey home, survived great hunger, a wolf attack, and the birth of her baby. "She cleared a hollow in the sand, gathered some firewood and built a fire. . . . She also brought some big flat rocks and put them into hot ashes. She placed the rocks and ashes under her. . . . While she massaged her abdomen, she sang the sacred song for the safe arrival of the baby."[12] The thin child lived, but the weak mother had to abandon it. Students' relatives will also tell them of having to make painful decisions for survival.

Specific topics sometimes help authors to focus their writing. For example,

---

[7]Frank B. Linderman, *Pretty-Shield* (Lincoln: University of Nebraska Press, 1973), p. 35.
[8]Jane B. Katz, *I Am the Fire of Time: The Voices of Native American Women* (New York: E. P. Dutton, 1977), p. 30.
[9]*Ibid.*, p. 80.
[10]John Lame Deer, *Lame Deer Seeker of Visions* (New York: Simon and Schuster, 1972), p. 13.
[11]*Ibid.*, p. 16.
[12]Broderick Johnson, *Navajo Stories of the Long Walk Period* (Tsaile: Navajo Community College Press, 1973), p. 71.

"A Violent Time" usually evokes powerful images. One model is the account of White Bull, a warrior who claimed he killed Custer. "I grabbed him and killed him. (*Le iya warpa ye na wokate lo tokeya wakteyelo.* . . .) I counted first coup. He hit me with his fists and hurt me and then he grabbed my braids. I grabbed his carbine and killed him. . . . The soldier was Long Hair."[13] White Bull's pictographs and the Sioux text are fascinating. Good writing should capture the instant flash of the drama. After reading White Bull's account, Virgil White Shirt relived his fight with a classmate: "He hit me. I hit him back. Then his fist missed my face, for I was too slick, sly, and wicked!"[14]

Students see themselves on paper and slowly trust their written words. N. Scott Momaday, Pulitzer Prize winner, explains this link: "I have said it. I have set it down. I trace the words and they stand for me." Momaday's memoir, *The Names*, is an album of cameo portraits. Students may emulate his eye for details. His grandfather was a sheriff: "It was a dangerous job; he shot at people, and people shot at him. It delighted me . . . that he slept with a pistol under his pillow." Momaday's father was a handsome swain in the 1920s. "My father is at the wheel of a new green pickup, and I am sitting beside him hugely pleased to be along. . . . My dog Blackie is at the rear window, riding high to the wind, laughing at me. . . . The little truck bounces over the dirt roads of the Navajo reservation, raises a great rooster tail of red dust."[15]

Like "an eyelash of eternity," Momaday's grandmother is history and legend in *The Way to Rainy Mountain*. "The last time I saw her she prayed standing by the side of her bed at night, naked to the waist, the light of a kerosene lamp moving upon her dark skin. Her long, black hair always drawn and braided in the day, lay upon her shoulders and against her breasts like a shawl . . . in the dancing light, she seemed beyond the reach of time . . . I think I knew then that I should not see her again."[16] Momaday says, in a sense, that we are all made of words. To extend his metaphor—autobiography is the flesh of family history. The student who transforms memory into words is saying, "I am history!"

---

[13]James H. Howard, ed., *The Warrior Who Killed Custer* (Lincoln: University of Nebraska Press, 1968), p. 55.
[14]Student paper in the author's possession.
[15]N. Scott Momaday, *The Names* (New York: Harper & Row, 1976), pp. 22, 67.
[16]N. Scott Momaday, *The Way to Rainy Mountain* (New York: Ballantine Books, 1970), p. 12.

WORKS CITED

Anderson, Robert. *Voices from Wounded Knee*. Rooseveltown: Akwesasne Notes, 1975.
Bataille, Gretchen M. *The Pretend Indians: Images of Native Americans in the Movies*. Ames: University of Iowa Press, 1980.
Brown, Dee. *Bury My Heart at Wounded Knee*. New York: Holt, Rinehart & Winston, Inc., 1970.
Costo, Rupert, ed. *Textbooks and the American Indian*. San Francisco: The Indian Historian Press, 1970.
Dorris, Michael, *Native Americans: 500 Years After*. New York: Crowell, 1975.
Erdoes, Richard. *The Sun Dance People*. New York: Vintage, 1972.
FitzGerald, Frances. *America Revised*. New York: Random House, 1980.
Highwater, Jamake, ed. *Song from the Earth: American Indian Painting*. Boston: New York Graphic Society, 1976.
Honour, Hugh. *The New Golden Land: European Images of America from Discoveries to the Present Time*. New York: Pantheon Books, 1975.
Howard, James H. *The Warrior Who Killed Custer*. Lincoln: University of Nebraska Press, 1968.
_____. *Indians, The First Americans*. New York: Scholastic Magazines, Inc., 1975.
Johnson, Broderick, ed. *Navajo Stories from the Long Walk Period*. Tsaile: Navajo Community College Press, 1973.
Katz, Jane B. *I Am the Fire of Time: Voices of Native American Women*. New York: E.P. Dutton, 1977.
Lame Deer, John. *Lame Deer, Seeker of Visions*. New York: Simon and Schuster, 1972.
Linderman, Frank B. *Pretty-Shield*. Lincoln: University of Nebraska Press, 1932.
Meinhardt, Nick. "Reviewing U.S. Treaty Commitments to the Lakota Nation." *American Indian Journal* 4 (January 1978): 2-12.
Neihardt, John. *Black Elk Speaks*. New York: William Morrow & Co., 1932.
Momaday, N. Scott. *The Names*. New York: Harper & Row, 1976.
_____. *The Way to Rainy Mountain*. New York: Ballantine Books, 1970.
Ortiz, Roxanne E. *The Great Sioux Nation*. Berkeley: University of California Press, 1977.
Powell, J.W., Director. "Lone Dog's Winter Count." *Tenth Annual Report of the Bureau of Ethnology*. Washington, D.C.: The Smithsonian Institution, 1893.
_____. *Proceedings of the Great Peace Commission of 1867-1868*. Washington, D.C.: The Institute for the Development of Indian Law, 1975.

Sandoz, Mari. *The Battle of the Little Big Horn*. Philadelphia: J.B. Lippincott, 1966.

_____. *Crazy Horse, Strange Man of the Oglalas*. New York: Alfred A. Knopf, 1972.

Scholder, Fritz. *Indian Kitsch*. Flagstaff, Northland Press, 1979.

Stereotypes, Distortions and Omissions in U.S. History Textbooks. New York: Council on Interracial Books for Children, Inc., 1977.

Treaties and Agreements of the Tribes and Bands of the Sioux Nation. Washington, D.C.: Institute for the Development of Indian Law, 1975.

Utley, Robert. "The Battle of the Little Big Horn." *Great Western Indian Fights*. Garden City: Doubleday and Co., 1960.

_____. *The Last Days of the Sioux Nation*. New Haven: Yale University Press, 1963.

Vestal, Stanley. *Sitting Bull*. Boston: Houghton Mifflin, 1932.

INDEX

Aid to families with dependent children, 36.
Afro-American, history, 2, 29; slaves, 75. *See also* Black; Slavery; Slaves.
Age-segregation, 32.
American Federation of Labor, 77.
American Indians. *See* Native Americans.
American Labor Union, 77.
Antislavery movement, 11.
Apache, 105.
Apprentices, 76.
Artisans, 74, 76, 78, 83.
Asylums, for the insane, 36.
Athabascan, 109.

Baby boom, 31, 33, 37.
Birth control, 6, 18. *See also* Contraception, Family-planning; Fertility; National Birth Control League.
Birth, rates, 20; records, 28.
Black Hills settlement, 94, 107, 108.
Black, community, 31; family life, 28, 29, 47–49; history, 1, 11, 51, 80; labor force, 75; women, 12. *See also* Afro-American; Slavery; Slaves.
Bureau of Indian Affairs, 91.

Central shop, 76, 85–86.
Cherokee, 93, 97, 99, 100.
Child labor. *See* Labor, child.
Childbearing, 37; history of, 53.
Childhood, history of, 58, 65, 66.
Childrearing, history of, 1, 54, 58, 66, 67–70; in Black families, 47–49; modern, 58; older forms of, 58; practices, 55; shared responsibility for, 31; women's role in, 10, 13, 14, 35, 36; years, 33.
Cloth production, 8. *See also* Spinning; Weaving.
Coeducation, 12.
Cohorts of families, 37, 38.
Colleges, for women, 10, 12.
Colonial, family, 43; period, 11. *See also* Women, colonial and revolutionary period.
Comanche, 105.

Competitive individualism, 74.
Conquest ideology, 98.
Consumers, 83; women as, 7.
Contraception, 11, 20. *See also* Birth control.
Cooking, 9. *See also* Food.
Craft, union, 77; workers, 74.
Crime, 56, 47, 65.
Criminology, 55.
Crow, 108.
"Cult of domesticity," 11, 12.
"Cult of true womanhood," 11. *See also* "True woman."

Dawes Severalty Act, 99.
Death, 32, 33, 34, 44; child, 58; infant, 45; rates, 33; records, 28. *See also* Mortality.
Depression of the 1930s, 37, 55.
Disease, 32.
Division of labor. *See* Labor, division of.
Divorce, 9, 32, 33, 44; rates, 20, 33, 49.
Domestic, labor, 12; service, 12; system of production, 83 (*see also* Household, as unit of production); tasks, 31.
Domestics, 79.
Domesticity, 11, 35.

Employer, 76, 77.
Employment, opportunity, 27; discrimination, 29, 36. *See also* Labor; Women, employment of; Work; Workers.
Enlightenment, 53, 55.
Equal Rights Amendment, 13, 18, 24.
Ethnic, backgrounds, 38; characteristics, 51; diversity, 10; experiences, 108; groups, 12; history, 1, 2, 51; rivalry, 79.
Ethnicity, 79.
Evangelical Protestantism, 75.
Extended family. *See* Family, extended.

Factories, 7, 8, 10, 55.
Factory, girl, 76; owners, 83 (*see also* Owners, industrial); system, 65, 75, 85–86; workers, 10, 52, 74, 75, 79, 88.
Family, 24; behavior, 55; cohorts (*see*

113

Cohorts of families); extended, 27, 30, 32, 56; firm, 77; history of, 2, **27–49**, 51, 64, 65, 80; life, 64, 66; nuclear, 28, 29, 30, 31, 32, 34, 56; size, 41, 45.
Family-planning, 37, 41. *See also* Birth control.
Farmers, 76.
Fertility, 11, 14, 31, 37. *See also* Birth control.
Fetterman Massacre, 107.
Fifteenth Amendment, 11.
Food, 8. *See also* Cooking.
Food stamps, 36.
Foreman, 77.
Fort Laramie Treaty of 1868, 106, 107, 108.
Fourteenth Amendment, 11.

General stores, 76.
Gilded Age, 74, 75.
Gold, discovery of, 101, 108.
Gospel of Wealth, 75.

Health, 57, 65, 66.
Health care, history of, 1, 51, 53, 54.
Helping professions, 35, 36.
Hispanics, history of, 1.
Home, 35, 76.
Hopi, 109.
Household, 7, 76; as unit of production, 76, 85–86; colonial, 8, 10; composition, 30, 38; one- or two-person, 32; population, 20; single-parent, 33; size, 17, 38; three-generation, 29, 30, 31; women's contribution to, 7, 8, 9, 13.
Housekeeping, 9.
Housework, 14.
Housewives, 53.

Images, of Native Americans, 91, 104.
Immigrants, 12, 31, 75, 77.
Immigration, 1, 20, 80.
Indentured servants, 74.
Indian Claims Commission, 100.
Indian New Deal, 100.
Indian Reorganization Act, 100.
Indians, American. *See* Native Americans.
Indian-White relations, 95, 96, 98, 103, 105.
Industrial, age, 10; economy, 29; jobs, 77; system, 31.
Industrial Revolution, 65, 71.
Industrialization, 28, 30, 65.
Insane, care for the, 36.
Insurance, 34.
Intertribal, issues, 96; politics, 97; relationships, 95, 96.
Intratribal issues, 96.

Irish, canal-diggers, 75; women, 12.
Iroquois, 97.
Italians, 79.

Jacksonian democracy, 55.
Job security, 34.
Journeymen, 76, 77, 84.

Kinship, 31, 35, 47.
Kiowa, 105.
Knights of Labor, 74.

Labor, child, 84; division of, 76, 77; domestic, 12; history of, 2, 13, 18, 52, 73–89; leaders, 73; movements, 74, 77; organization, 78; unions, 2, 73, 77, 78, 79, 83, 84, 88–89.
Labor-saving devices, 13.
Laguna, 105.
Laissez-faire economics, 75.
Lakota, 93, 94, 107.
Leisure, 71; activities, 57, 59; history of, 54; patterns of, 65.
Life expectancy, 17, 20. *See also* Longevity.
Little Big Horn, Battle of the, 105, 107, 108.
Longevity, 31. *See also* Life expectancy.
Lowell millworkers, 74, 78.

Management, 75.
Marriage, 24, 37, 47, 49, 76; rates, 20, 32; records, 28.
Marriage-age, 41, 45; of women, 9.
Mass production, 76.
Matriarchs, tribal, 8.
Medical care, 57; history of, 58, 65. *See also* Health; Health care.
Medicare, 36.
Mexican-Americans, 12.
"Middle passage of U.S. industrialism," 76.
Monopoly, 77, 79.
Mortality, 32, 33, 57. *See also* Death.
Mother, woman as, 10; working, 14, 49.
Motherhood, 10.
Moynihan Report, 28.

National Birth Control League, 18. *See also* Birth control.
National Women's Party, 13, 18.
Native Americans, history of, 1, 2, **91–112**.
Navajo, 109, 110.
Needle trades, 12. *See also* Sewing.
"New Indian History," 92, 94, 96, 97, 98, 101.
"New Indians," 91.
"New social history," 27, 40.
Nez Percé, 100, 101.

INDEX

Nineteenth Amendment, 13, 25. *See also* Suffrage movement.
Nuclear family. *See* Family, nuclear.

Oral history traditions, 94, 96, 97, 100, 101, 107.
Organized labor. *See* Labor, unions.
Owners, industrial, 75. *See also* Factory, owners.

Polish, immigrants, male, 12; women, 12.
Preindustrial age, 10, 65; patterns of work and leisure, 65, 75.
Primary workers, 36.
Puritanism, 6.
Puritans, 98.

Red Cloud's War, 107.
"Red power," 91.
Retirement, 70–71.
Romantic love, 28, 29.
Romanticism, 53.

Secondary workers, 36.
Seneca, 97, 98.
Sewing, 9. *See also* needle trades.
Sewing machine, invention of, 6, 13, 76.
Sex roles, 37, 79.
Sex-role definitions, 7. *See also* Sexual stereotypes.
Sexual behavior, history of, 1, 53.
Sexual habits, 55.
Sexual stereotypes, 19, 20. *See also* Sex roles; Sex-role definitions.
Sheppard-Towner Maternity Bill, 18.
Shoemakers, 76, 83–84.
Shoemaking, 75, 83–84.
Sioux, 106, 107, 108, 110.
Slavery, 10, 12, 28, 47, 49, 75; history of, 2, 52.
Slaves, 74, 75, 99.
Slavic, coal miners, 79; steelworkers, 75.
Social feminism, 13.
Social history, 1, 2, 3, 16, **51–71**.
Social security, 36.
Spinning, 7. *See also* Cloth production.
Steel industry, 77.
Stereotypes, of Native Americans, 93, 106.
Success ideology, 74.
Suffrage, women's, 13, 24; movement, 11, 13, 16.

Swaddling, 58, 67, 68.

Ten Hour Petitions, 78.
Terence Powderly Papers, 74.
Tribal, governments, 108; history, 96, 100, 103; life, 97; memory, 94.
Tribe, 96.
"True Woman," 35. *See also* "Cult of true womanhood,"
Typewriter, invention of, 6.

Unions, labor. *See* Labor, unions.
Urban, areas, 10; Black, 53; workingmen, 78.
Urbanization, 1, 28.

Wage-earning, 9, 12. *See also* Wages; Work; Women, employment of; Women, working.
Wages, 35, 76, 79. *See also* Wage-earning.
Weaving, 7. *See also* Cloth production.
Welsh miners, 75.
Wet-nursing, 58, 68.
White-Indian relations. *See* Indian-White relations.
Women, colonial and revolutionary period, 7–10; employment of, 7, 12, 14, 19-23; history of, 1, 2, 5-25, 51, 80; nineteenth-century, 10–13; twentieth-century, 13–14; working, 9, 10, 12, 74, 78. *See also* Suffrage; Women's rights movement; Work; Workers.
Women's Bureau of the Department of Labor, 13.
Women's rights movement, 11. *See also* Suffrage.
Women's studies, 16.
Work, 35, 64, 65, 71, 73, 76, 86; as part of family life, 27; ethic, 75; outside the home, 9, 14, 36, 42; women's 11, 12, 51. *See also* Employment; Labor; Women; Workers; Workplace.
Worker, 73, 75, 76.
Workers, 35, 74, 75, 76, 77, 83, 85, 86; blue-collar, 1; factory, 10; women, 13, 78.
Working-class, 73, 78, 79.
Workplace, 73, 76, 77.
Wounded Knee, 1890 massacre at, 107; 1973 siege of, 91, 107.

OTHER NCSS PUBLICATIONS RELATED TO THE TEACHING OF AMERICAN HISTORY

**VALUES OF THE AMERICAN HERITAGE:
CHALLENGES, CASE STUDIES, AND TEACHING STRATEGIES**
Carl Ubbelohde & Jack R. Fraenkel, Editors
Explores American values. Case studies of impressment of seamen, trial of Susan B. Anthony, Mormon experiences, and Standard Oil Company.
214 pp. $8.75   1976

**TEACHING ABOUT WOMEN IN THE SOCIAL STUDIES:
CONCEPTS, METHODS, AND MATERIALS**
Jean Dresden Grambs, Editor
Valuable publication for teaching about women in U.S. History, World History, and other courses. Guidelines for selecting instructional materials.
119 pp. $5.95   1976

**TEACHING AMERICAN HISTORY:
THE QUEST FOR RELEVANCY**
Allan O. Kownslar, Editor
Specific, practical, and class-tested lessons designed to relate the American past to the needs of today's students.
237 pp. $6.95   1974

TEACHING ETHNIC STUDIES
James A. Banks, Editor
Outstanding yearbook with major sections on teaching about Asian Americans, Blacks, Chicanos, Native Americans, Puerto Ricans, White Ethnics and Women.
300 pp. $7.20   1973

**THE REINTERPRETATION OF
AMERICAN HISTORY AND CULTURE**
William H. Cartwright and Richard L. Watson, Jr., Editors
Distinguished scholars discuss interpretations of American history from colonial times to the present.
554 pp. $8.50   1973

Production: Elizabeth Qualls
Editorial Assistance: Anita Draper
Cover: Bill Caldwell